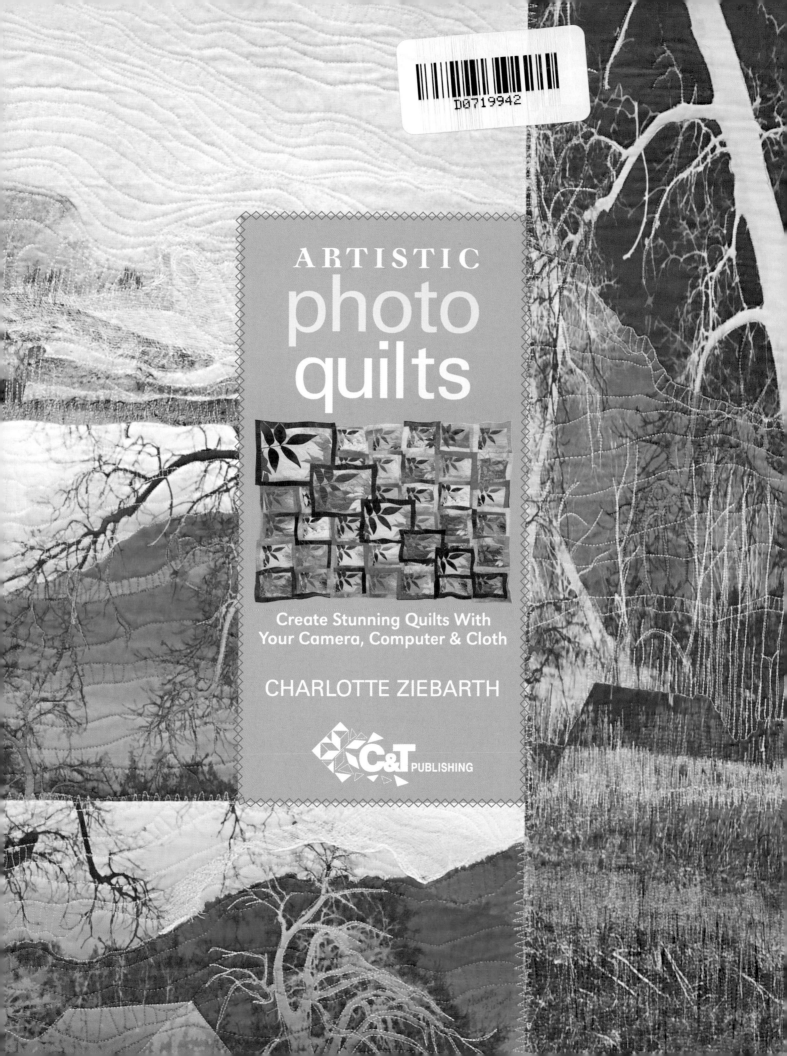

ARTISTIC
photo
quilts

Create Stunning Quilts With Your Camera, Computer & Cloth

CHARLOTTE ZIEBARTH

C&T PUBLISHING

Text: © 2009 by Charlotte Ziebarth

Artwork: © 2009 by C&T Publishing, Inc.

Publisher: Amy Marson

Creative Director: Gailen Runge

Editors: Lynn Koolish and Cynthia Bix

Technical Editor: Sandy Peterson

Copyeditor/Proofreader: Wordfirm Inc.

Cover Designer/Book Designer: Christina D. Jarumay

Production Coordinators: Tim Manibusan and Kirstie L. Pettersen

Quilt photography by Christina Carty-Francis and Diane Pedersen of C&T Publishing, Inc.; all other photography by Charlotte Ziebarth unless otherwise noted.

Published by C&T Publishing, Inc., P.O. Box 1456, Lafayette, CA 94549

Library of Congress Cataloging-in-Publication Data

Ziebarth, Charlotte

Artistic photo quilts : create stunning quilts with your camera, computer & cloth / Charlotte Ziebarth.

   p. cm.

Includes bibliographical references and index.

Summary: "An in-depth look at the working process for creating digitally altered photography, printing it onto cloth, and making wall art quilts, with emphasis on nurturing the reader's own creativity"—Provided by publisher.

ISBN 978-1-57120-600-8 (paper trade : alk. paper)

1. Photography—Digital techniques. 2. Textile printing. 3. Adobe Photoshop Elements. 4. Quilting. I. Title.

TR267.5.A33Z54 2009

746.46—dc22

                                    2008050944

Printed in China

10 9 8 7 6 5 4 3 2

ACKNOWEDGMENTS

I would like to acknowledge all my weaving and quilting friends and colleagues over the years, because I have learned many things from all of them.

I want to thank especially the other members of Piecemakers for friendship and critical help, laughs, good food and hospitality, and stimulating times: Faye Anderson, Jamie Bolane, Diana Bunnell, Betsy Cannon, Barbara Cohen, Helen Davis, Lynda Faires, Patty Hawkins, Gretchen Hill, Judith Trager, and Carol Watkins.

If it weren't for the Front Range Contemporary Quilters, both the members and the fabulous artist/teachers they have brought to Colorado over the last fifteen years, I would probably not be a quilting artist today. Thank you especially to Sue Benner and Pauline Burbidge for teaching me about fusing and innovative quilt construction techniques.

Thanks to Lynn Koolish, Jan Grigsby, and others at C&T who had faith I could do this book.

And of course my greatest thanks go to my partner, husband, and friend, Ken, for putting up with me all these years and being a champion of my artwork.

contents

introduction

Harmony, 50″ × 13″, 2007

I have done quilting and other fiber work for many years. Photography was always a sideline to my artwork, serving as an inspiration source. When I learned how to print photographs on fabric, photography truly became integrated into my artwork. Many people have used the printing technology to print family photos on cloth to put into quilts. I began by using my nature photography in my quilts. As I learned digital alteration of photographs, I began taking pictures not only of things I loved but also of things that would make a useful layer or background in my digital compositions—pictures of peeling paint, interesting cracks in the pavement, or drippy rust patterns. Photography became one of the principal tools in my artwork.

Rock line photo used in *Harmony*

Water on roof

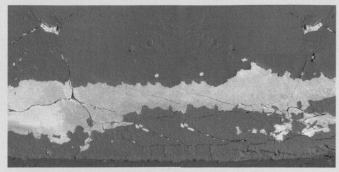

Peeling paint used in *Birds in the Bush* (page 76)

As the process evolved, I found that I was creating my own computer-designed images, not merely printing a photograph onto fabric. Although I use photography, it has become just the **first step** in the design process. The question of how I could alter photographs became more interesting than simply printing the photograph itself. The making of the quilt became an exploration of image possibilities at several stages in the process.

This book will describe what I have learned as I began to explore changing and altering photographs to use in my quilt work. It is not meant to be a step-by-step, do-exactly-what-I-did type of book. I hope it will point the way for you to learn how to turn your photographs into unique images for your artwork, whether you are making quilts or some other type of artwork.

Although it is possible to totally design all of the artwork on the computer, the cloth and stitching and other art media interact with the printed images in interesting, often surprising ways. The process of discovery and not knowing exactly how a quilt will look until it is finished is what keeps me interested. The more opportunities for serendipity and improvisation along the way, the better.

How to Use This Book

I use Adobe Photoshop Elements software for my artwork, although any good photo-editing software can be used. Menu and feature locations within different Photoshop Elements versions may vary slightly from this text, but the functionality is there. Explore!

While this book doesn't include the beginning basics for Photoshop Elements, there are many sources for beginners, so don't worry about that. There are books and online tutorials, including C&T Publishing's Photoshop Elements Basics (www.ctpub.com). There is also a *Help* drop-down command within Photoshop Elements to answer basic questions. Or consult the online help in your photo-editing software. Even if you haven't used Photoshop Elements before, these resources make things easy to learn.

This book gives you easy tips and methods for transforming your photos into artful creations. The chapters include design exercises that help you play with your creations. Following basic techniques covered in this book, you can create artistic prints without prior knowledge of the software. There is room to expand your boundaries by reading and learning more, or just by experimenting with the techniques described.

Once you get started transforming your photos, you'll be addicted, so don't hesitate to get started. Grab your camera and sense of adventure, and join me on the journey of discovery.

photography and **computers**

computers and software

I use sewing machines, cameras, computers, printers, scanners, needles, and paint brushes to make my art. It is easy to think that the type of camera or printer you use will make a major difference to your art, but these are just tools. Technical concerns often overwhelm the creative process when you are dealing with computers, printers, and digital cameras. Concern for the art produced should take precedence. Bigger and better equipment does not make a better photographer, digital artist, or quilter.

It doesn't matter what kind of computer you are using. The main thing to remember is that digital photos and digital manipulations use a lot of memory and storage, so you need a machine with a lot of each. This will not be a problem unless you are using an older computer.

All of the work in this book was done with Adobe Photoshop Elements software (hereafter referred to in this book as Photoshop Elements). It is inexpensive, easy to learn, and quite powerful. Periodically, free trial copies of this editing software are available online (see Resources on page 94). You do not need to buy the very expensive Photoshop CS or other software to do interesting things. If image-editing software came with your camera or computer, learn to use it. Corel's Paint Shop Pro is easy to use and has the same type of capabilities as Photoshop Elements. Eventually you may want one of the more advanced programs, but you can do a lot with the simpler software, and you might find it more accessible in the beginning.

If you are very new to using image-editing software, look for one of the many books that start with the basics, such as Gregory Georges' *50 Fast Digital Photo Techniques*. Two other books aimed specifically at quilters are Beth Wheeler and Lori Marquette's *Altered Photo Artistry* and Cyndy Rymer and Lynn Koolish's *Innovative Fabric Imagery for Quilts,* both of which deal with simple image editing and printing on fabric. The DVD *Lynn Koolish Teaches You Printing on Fabric* includes Photoshop Elements basics, as well as printing on fabric basics.

You don't necessarily need to take a class. I think the best way to learn to use these image-editing programs is to play with them. Go through all the menu options and tools and try them on your photographs. It can be very exciting to discover on your own what you can do with your photographs. Use the *Help* drop-down menu in your software. There are also many online tutorials and forums for many of the digital altering programs. Also check C&T Publishing's website for Photoshop Elements Basics (www.ctpub.com). Be warned—it is great fun and quite addictive!

> **TIP**
> Before exploring Photoshop Elements, select a photograph to experiment with, save it as a new name, and have fun trying things out. With the photo saved as a new name, you don't have to worry about making mistakes on the original.

> **TIP**
> For simplicity, Photoshop Elements commands are abbreviated as follows: *Filters>Artistic>Cutout,* which tells you to go to the *Filters* menu and drag down to the *Artistic* command and drag over and down to the *Cutout* command. On-screen tools, buttons, and icons will also be italicized.

digital cameras

Although, of course, you can use any camera or any type of photograph as the basis for digital artwork, I have found that the digital camera changed my photography, changed my view of myself as a photographer, and led me to use my photographs directly in my artwork. I love the ease of taking pictures experimentally, and taking lots of them, without committing to the expense of developing or printing any of them. Taking photographs has become a kind of artistic note taking and image capturing that is only a first step in the artistic process. I have many photos of green ash leaves on the branch so I can study their line patterns. Some have inspired quilts.

Simple leaf photographs and some of their digital alterations

Purple Ash Leaves, a mini-quilt, 11″ × 8″, 2006

MEGAPIXELS

People tend to be impressed with large megapixel numbers on new cameras. While it is possible to buy 12- and 14-megapixel cameras, you don't need to have high-resolution files when you are printing on cloth. Photos taken with a 4- or 5-megapixel camera are fine. Even when printing on larger pieces of cloth, you do not need large file sizes. In fact, all of the initial photographs used for the quilts in this book were taken with cameras of 5 megapixels or fewer.

The larger the file size you use when taking photographs, the more storage the photos need on your computer, CD, or other storage device. When you have taken many digital photographs, this storage can become an issue, so think carefully before routinely taking many photos larger than 5 or 6 megapixels.

Working with large photograph files can be cumbersome because digital effects take longer to process as well as using more computer storage.

CAMERA WEIGHT

If your camera is small and lightweight, you will be more likely to take it with you in your purse, briefcase, or pack, or around your neck, without its becoming burdensome. Rechargeable batteries are a must, and it helps to carry extra charged batteries as well as extra memory cards. Or if your cell phone has a camera, it is great for those emergency photographs. Even a 1-megapixel camera photograph can be used as a basis for digital transformations.

LCD Screens

Many photographers prefer single-lens reflex (SLR) digital cameras, but they are heavier and more complex, especially with a long zoom lens attached. If you want to keep the picture-taking process as simple as possible, this may not be the best camera for regular use. Composing your pictures on the LCD screen of a smaller camera, especially with a screen that pivots, can have advantages. SLR cameras show you only the picture you have taken, not the picture you are composing on the LCD screen. While composing, you don't have to hold the camera up to your eye, which means you can take pictures from different viewpoints. It also functions as a people filter—you can hold the camera over your head or away from your body, zoom in on a subject viewed in your pivoted LCD screen, and not be bothered by the people in front of you.

Many photographers don't like the difficulties of using these LCD screens in bright sunlight, which can be a problem, especially when combined with sunglasses. In these conditions you need the viewfinder, so it is nice to have both options.

Zoom and Macro Capabilities

A camera with a 12x optical zoom and built-in image stabilizer is nice to have because it allows you to zoom in on faraway subjects and record more details with minimal camera shake, even if you don't use a tripod. Additionally, a camera with a good macro lens capability will enable you to get very close to subjects such as leaves and flowers. A simple close-up looking into a crocus flower produced *Saffron Symmetry*.

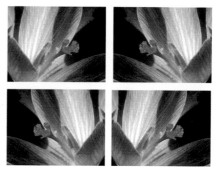

Crocus flower photo in four orientations

Close-up of a crocus

Details of *Saffron Symmetry*

Saffron Symmetry, 49″ × 21″, 2005

using a scanner as a camera

A flatbed scanner (or all-in-one printer, copier, and scanner) is a very useful tool in the digital composition process. Drawings or paintings, small watercolors, found objects, and all manner of copyright-free material can be scanned and added to a composition. This is also a good way to use old or pre-digital printed photographs. See *Blue Hills* (page 72) and *Migration Dream #1* (page 84) for uses of scanned watercolor paintings in digital designs for quilts.

You can have great fun scanning sliced vegetables, lettuce leaves, small objects, colorful autumn leaves, and flowers. Be sure to remove the items and clean your scanner glass after using these natural things. During the making of *Leafy Green Salad*, my husband opened the scanner lid to copy a document and was surprised by four-day-old decomposing spinach leaves!

Scanned lettuce image

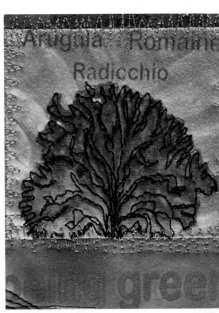

Details of *Leafy Green Salad*

Leafy Green Salad, 24″ × 24″, 2001

photography as a tool

Photography is a tool for your creative fiber work as well as an artistic focus. You do not have to be a professional photographer to have good images to use in your quilts. A photograph does not have to be perfect. It does not have to be startling or provocative. It does not have to be the most beautiful photograph ever taken to be useful in your artwork. It can be a very ordinary picture. In fact, most of my digital creations started with very simple, very ordinary photographs, not gorgeous, wonderful photographs.

simple pictures often work best

Simple unassuming pictures yield interesting results once you start playing in the digital darkroom. This robin picture was the basis for the images used in *Return of the Robins* (page 49). In and of itself it is not really a very interesting picture, but I was able to use it to create something quite beautiful. Even some of the extraneous lines turned out to create interesting effects. None of the lines or background was edited out.

Altered image used in *Return of the Robins* (See pages 69–70 for an explanation of the image alterations.)

Another image used in creating *Return of the Robins*

Original robin photo

How Many Pixels

As mentioned earlier, a photograph does not need a huge number of pixels to be used. To show you an example, this picture of a bicycle was derived from a very low-resolution scan of a small print because I had only a 2 × 2-inch print of the photo. The photo would not be acceptable as a larger print on paper, because there are not enough pixels—it would be blurry and have jagged pixel edges. But as a hazy image incorporated into other compositions, it works just fine and has a soft quality that is pleasing. It was used in many quilts, including *Spirals and Trees #13*.

Original scan of bicycle photo

Detail from *Spirals and Trees #13*

Spirals and Trees #13, 23″ × 19″, 2003

Bad Pictures Can Often Be Useful

This grainy and distant picture of cranes flying in to land at the Bosque del Apache Wildlife Refuge in New Mexico became the large and enhanced crane image used in *Under a Blue Cloud* and has been used in many ways in other quilts. Once in the computer, images can be transformed to different sizes and colors.

Grainy photo of cranes

Detail from *Cranes and Clouds #3* (page 78)

Under a Blue Cloud, 35″ × 25″, 2006

Images as Templates or Stencils

Simple images are also good for making templates or stencils to cut out a shape from another printed fabric, as in *Bird Thoughts II,* where some of the bird shapes were cut out of printed tree fabric. To make a template or stencil, trace the shape onto freezer paper (or to the paper side of paper-backed fusible web), iron it to the printed fabric, and cut it out. Fabric is much easier to cut when it has paper or fusible web adhered to it. For more information about the digitally altered tree image used in *Bird Thoughts II,* see Deidre's Tree (pages 66–68).

Blackbird in a tree

Bird Thoughts II, 28˝ × 21˝, 2003, private collection

LOOK FOR HIGH CONTRAST

A high-contrast picture with a simple background works very well in digital compositions. This cottonwood tree, taken in winter with a slightly foggy background, served as a basis for many tree digital manipulations and has been used in many quilts.

Original photograph of cottonwood tree

Tree selected from background and duplicated smaller on left side

Trees layered with clouds (see page 79)

Another Fine Day, 45″ × 24″, 2004

Detail from *Another Fine Day*

Another high-contrast photo I have used is this silhouette image of trees along the coastline in Padstow, Cornwall, England.

Original photo of trees

Altered image ready to use in quilt

This brings up another point. Of the 700 pictures I took on that trip to England, this is the only one I have used on a quilt so far. The photographs you use in your artwork might be quite different from the usual family and vacation photographs. Although I have many pictures from interesting places where I have traveled, it has been the photographs taken close to home that I have used most in my quilt artwork.

Disguised Contrast

When you are taking a photo, you don't always see what later becomes important. In the fence photos below, the fence wires reflecting winter sunshine show up more in the altered photograph than in the original. Those fence lines were not really what I was photographing; in fact, I didn't even notice their strong appearance until I started altering the photo. The wires became more substantial and quite unlike the original when altered in the digital darkroom. The altered photo was the basic photo used in *Beyond the Fence #1.*

Original fence photo   **Altered photo**

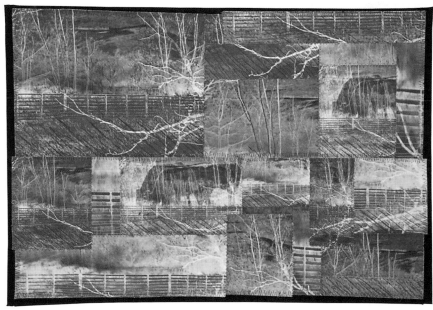

Beyond the Fence #1, 36˝ × 24˝, 2007

> **TIP**
>
> Learn to pay attention to extreme darks and lights when you are taking photos. This results in a strong photo and also is very powerful in digital alterations.

OUT-OF-FOCUS AREAS

Photographs with large out-of-focus areas are good candidates for digital darkroom manipulations because they leave interesting and mysterious places in the digital canvas. This photo, with a large out-of-focus area, contributed to the interesting outlines and images in the Maple Magic design study below. The photo is a reflection of leaves in a birdbath. The layering technique is described on pages 63–64.

Original photo

Maple Magic design study using layers of the photo

take many photographs

Take a lot of photos so you will have a lot of choices when it comes time to design on the computer. With a digital camera it is easy and cheap to take many, many views of a subject. Photos of commonplace objects can be quite useful, but also be on the lookout for unusual things to photograph. Take your camera with you everywhere: the zoo, a greenhouse, a hardware store, a parking lot, anywhere and everywhere. Two books for thinking about photography that I particularly like are Freeman Patterson's *Photography and the Art of Seeing* and David Finn's *How to Look at Everything*.

TAKE DIFFERENT VIEWS

A good habit to develop is to shoot your subject from many different viewpoints: zoomed in as close as you can get, from a distance, from the right, from the left, with different backgrounds, and so on. Be sure to shoot lots of details. Use your camera to study the object. The more choices you have when it comes time to play at the computer, the better. Think of it as making a thorough study of the subject, taking visual notes on all aspects. The photo montage of Virginia creeper vines shows 16 different pictures (of the 100 or more that I have taken at different times) of the gorgeous red vines growing along a wall

and up a tree trunk. Because I have taken so many different photos of these vines, I have lots of choice when designing the images in this quilt series. See page 91 for one of the quilts from this series.

Photo montage from journal

Virginia creeper vines

Photographic Study of a Common Object

Find a simple subject in your house or yard to photograph, and then try to take unusual angles, views, close-ups, and pairings with other objects or backgrounds. Ordinary everyday objects, really looked at and studied, can become interesting material for your work. Try the following:

■ Deliberately take some photos with out-of-focus areas.

■ Take photographs at different times of day for different lighting conditions.

■ Pair your object with different backgrounds.

■ Aim for at least 25 different views of your subject.

TAKE PHOTOS FOR THEIR COLORS

Another way to use your photographs is somewhat subtle— use them for printing simple colors and color gradations. A portion of a sunset sky cropped and enlarged can be a very nice color gradation. Used just for the color, a somewhat mottled and pixelated image is rather like a dyed, painted, or batik fabric. When used along with the original photos, it makes for interesting semisolid colors. These images often have more liveliness than the standard software solid color or color gradation. They also can be very useful when it comes to layering photographs (pages 58 and 70). Refer to the Color Collection Library (page 23) for an example of how to store these particular photos.

Sunset photo with portion of clouded sky to be enlarged

Enlarged photo detail

This badly out-of-focus picture nearly got deleted, but I decided it would provide a good, simple, non-object-related color gradation and should go into my color folder. It can be changed into any number of other colors and retain the soft color modulation.

Greenish-orange out-of-focus photo is good for color

Same photograph with altered color (page 55)

TAKE PHOTOS FOR THEIR PATTERNS

You can also print patterns—polka dots, stripes, animal skin textures, whatever. Use details from photos, altered photos, scanned paintings, and so on. These images can be useful printed as is or used as texture layers combined with other photos in digital alterations.

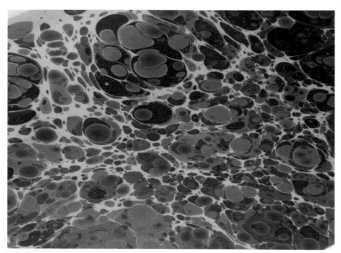

Photo from marbling demonstration

Water reflections

organizing the original photos

Organizing your photographs can be a challenging process to describe because there are so many ways to do it. Each photo downloading program has a different system. Photoshop Elements versions 3.0 and higher have a nice system called Photo Organizer that allows you to tag images with labels, which comes in very handy when you accumulate thousands of photos.

Store photos on the computer (with a backup hard drive) until you are ready to store them on CD or DVD. Store the photos in folders labeled by date, which is how many cameras and photo organizers download them. It is very helpful to have an added title to remind you what is there, especially if you are not tagging them right away.

If you are a very visual person and a book lover, you may enjoy storing prints of your photos in large albums. With Canon's PhotoRecord software or with the Photo Organizer software in Photoshop Elements, you can print index pages of all photographs (twenty 2 × 2-inch photos per page) and/or enlargements of your favorites. Print the photos on good paper, and place them in archival plastic page protectors. Label each page of prints with the date and title of the file where that photograph can be found so you can easily lay your hands on the digital version of the photo you see in the album. Many people will prefer not to do this, but I like being able to take my albums wherever I want to look at them and not being tied to the computer screen all the time.

SOURCE LIBRARY

Soon you will have so many digital photographs that it will be cumbersome to keep all your photos only on the hard drive or CDs and in the photo albums. I have found it very useful to have folders on my computer with copies of favorite photos or favorite themes. There are folders for subjects I have used, such as birds, cows, leaves, old buildings, water abstracts, tulips, sunsets, flowers, grasses, and so on. I also try to keep copies of the original photos used in each quilt design in computer folders categorized by that quilt's name and ultimate finish date.

> **TIP**
>
> Start a computer library of your favorite photographic subjects so they will be easy to find.

> **TIP**
>
> Keep copies of your favorite photographs together in the folders where you're going to use them, even if it means keeping duplicate copies. That way they'll be at your fingertips when you want to use them.

Examples from the author's Bird Source Collection

COLOR COLLECTION LIBRARY

Another way you can store copies of photos is by color. Collect examples in the twelve colors of the color wheel. Stored in a folder, these photos can give you ideas of images you might want to use in a quilt. The photos can be the source for printing large solid, gradational, or textured color fabrics described earlier (page 20).

Samples from the author's blue collection

Even easier is to let the software find colors for you. Photoshop Elements Organizer contains a *Find by Color Similarity* feature that allows you to find all the photographs in your collection that contain colors similar to a selected photograph. With this option, select the orange begonia blossom you just photographed, and it will find all the bright orange images you have on your computer. Newer versions of the software have this *Find by Visual Similarity* feature. You'll find it under *Photoshop Elements Organizer>Organize>Find>Find by Visual Similarity with Selected Photo(s)*.

EXERCISE 2
Organize Your Photos

ORGANIZE BY SUBJECT

Look through your favorite photographs and make collections of similar images you might want to use. Place copies of these digital photos into folders on your computer, or use a tagging system. The Photo Organizing software in Photoshop Elements will get you started with categories. Ultimately this will save you lots of time. If it seems like a daunting task, start with a few categories and add to them periodically.

ORGANIZE BY SPECIFIC USE IN A QUILT

When you are working on a particular quilt design, gather **copies** of the photos you think you might be using. Keep these copies along with the digitally altered ones all together, labeled with the quilt's working title and date started. Later, when the quilt is finished, you can change the folder's name to the final quilt name and date completed.

inspiration

where do ideas come from?

People often ask artists where we get our ideas. Every artist probably has a different answer or several answers. Our idea-generating process is as unique as our individual work. What inspires one person may not inspire another. Most of my ideas are generated from noticing and taking pictures of my environment, from seeing lots of art, from working in the studio, from actively working with my photographic images, and increasingly, from playing with the digital alteration software.

> **TIP**
>
> Pay attention to where you are and what you are doing when artwork ideas come to you. Write them down, sketch them, or photograph them. Make sure you revisit those places and repeat those activities often.

OBSERVING AND PHOTOGRAPHING

Inspiration can come from anywhere when you are carefully observing. By looking for things to photograph, you are forcing your brain into a different observational mode, different from your normal mode. Whether you take your inspiration from the natural world, from the landscapes around you, from the urban environment, from city parks and gardens, from sporting events or other places where people gather, or from traveling in interesting and beautiful places, photography can help you observe. Photographs can both **result from** your inspiration and **be** your inspiration.

Old Barn/South Boulder Creek, 20˝ × 34˝, 2002

Old barn photo

OTHER ARTISTS, PAST AND PRESENT

Inspiration also comes from seeing and reading about other people's art and other cultures' arts. Study art history books, exhibit catalogs, and books by and about artists and craftspeople. Visiting exhibits of both museum collections and contemporary art stimulates ideas. In addition to appreciating the images created by other artists, you learn how they make their art and how one piece of work leads to another. Hearing other artists talk about and show pictures of their work always gives insight into how they see the world, and stimulates artistic motivation, and often gives ideas about a direction in which your future work might proceed. Creativity can be infectious.

WORKING IN THE STUDIO

Many times ideas come while actually in the studio actively working. The process of sewing, drawing, and composing artwork generates more ideas about what to do next. I've taken to keeping a notepad by the sewing machine to jot down ideas that occur to me while in the contemplative mood that sewing or quilting encourages. Making art inspires more artwork ideas.

WORKING WITH THE IMAGES

Physically handling the visual images is extremely conducive to generating ideas and works in conjunction with designing on the computer. Rather than just looking at your photographs, if you resize them, crop them, rotate them, cut them out, and move them around, you generate ideas about artwork to make with some of these images.

For the *Sand Pictures* quilt series (one is shown on page 26) I made several different collages, but not all turned into quilts. The quilt series developed from pictures taken of Medano Creek at the Great Sand Dunes National Park. It is a shallow creek that can stop and start again after summer rains in the nearby mountains. Although there were more inspiring views and photos taken here, the foamy water starting to flow across the sand created fascinating abstract images, which I photographed in detail. I made several collages for my photo journal before I started altering the images on the computer.

Medano Creek after a rainstorm

Medano Creek photo journal montage

PLAYING WITH DIGITAL ALTERATION

As you learn to alter your photographs on the computer, you will find that you want to spend more and more time simply playing with the ways you can change your photographs and create new digital compositions. Seeing what happens to the images as you add one photo to another and change the way the photographs interact provides endless inspiration. Major work on quilt design evolves and develops during this play. And it **is** play. This is some of the best artistic fun you can have. You learn a lot *and* become inspired while playing.

Playing with the abstract foamy water pictures shown here, I changed their colors and blended some with others to create new and very different images. (Refer to page 58 for how the color changes were achieved.) The resulting quilt is an impression of a landscape that takes on a sense of mystery. The images evoke a feeling of other places. By playing with these images on the computer, I created an inspiration I didn't have when I started out.

Original photo of foamy water pattern

A color alteration of original photo

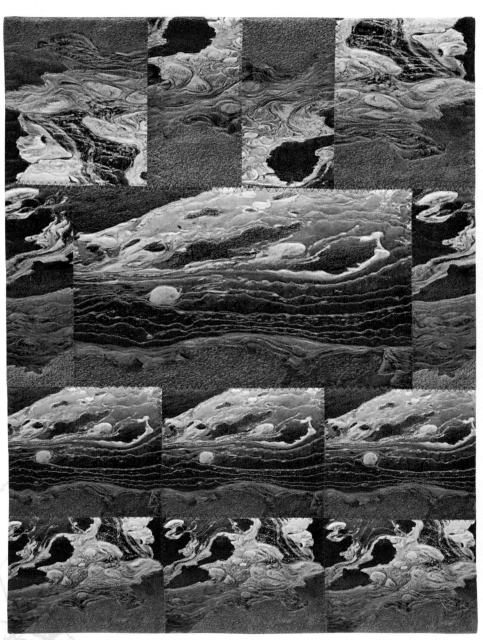

Medano Creek: Sand Pictures #2, 29″ × 37″, 2007

developing
personal themes

Everyone has favorite subjects for making art. Mine are continually evolving, but some elements remain the same: trees and leaves, landscapes and nature, abandoned buildings, abstract imagery in real objects, color relationships, and an obsession with linear elements. These are the things I continually photograph and make quilts about. Although beautiful landscape photographs inspire me, they are not necessarily the photos I use in the digital manipulations. I have used simpler images, such as Deidre's cottonwood tree (pages 66–68), in quilts to convey more mysterious and painterly imagery in quilts. *Cottonwood Rhapsody #1* is one example of how I used this simple tree photo.

Original photo (Deidre's cottonwood tree) for *Cottonwood Rhapsody #1*

TIP

Look at your photographs and your artwork, and make a list of the themes you see reflected. Consider how you might further explore them.

Cottonwood Rhapsody #1, 31˝ × 34˝, 2002

LANDSCAPE AND NATURE

"In all things of nature there is something of the marvelous." —Aristotle

Nature photography has always been a source of ideas for artwork. Use your photographs to see what it is that captures your interest in your environment—to see what it is that you see that other people might not see. Inspiration and photography can happen while walking around the block or in your yard. Even in the city there are bits of nature in the plantings and the parks. Trees, leaves, landforms, bark patterns, garden flowers, stones, and birds are everywhere.

Fall foliage

Stones in water

ABANDONED BUILDINGS

Things left behind and abandoned seem to retain an element of mystery. Who were the people who lived there or used these things? How did the world look to them? Time etches these things and creates new color, line, and shape interest.

Windows in old building

Open Windows, Open Spaces, 24″ × 24″, 2006

ABSTRACTION

*"Nothing is less real than realism....
It is only by selection, by elimination,
by emphasis, that we get at the real
meaning of things." —Georgia O'Keeffe*

Interesting abstract qualities that are
fascinating photographs as is exist everywhere, but they can also be altered,
combined, and rearranged. Often these
photos are good for adding a drawn
quality to your digital design. Sometimes
they are good examples of the organiza-
tion of spatial elements. Their interest
often lies beyond the reality of what
they are.

Ice pattern

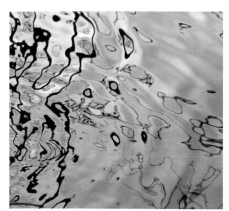

Water reflection patterns

COLOR

*"Color is one of the great things in the
world that makes life worth living...."*
—Georgia O'Keeffe

Many artists are obsessed with color. If
you salivate over any arrangement of colored objects—a row of paint chips at the
hardware store, a pile of yarns, or even
simple crayons—use this interest to stim-
ulate your creativity. Photography can
document color studies, color gradations,
color as contrast, and color relationships
of all kinds. Be on the lookout for striking
and unusual color combinations and
gradations from one color to another.
Document these with your photography
for later inspiration. Whether it is in gardens, fabric scraps, or sunsets, color is
often a main artistic passion.

Princess Diana Gardens in London, 2003

Fabric scraps

LINE

Line, as well as color, can be an inspiration. Line drawings can be found in
pictures of bare tree branches, snow lines,
architectural components, interesting
cracks and salt lines in the sidewalk,
peeling paint lines, or the echoing repeat
of lines in grassy plants. As quilters and
embroiderers, we are especially interested
in line.

Window reflections

Grasses on a pond

photo montage and design

My themes are reflected in the photo montages I create. Cutting, assembling, and arranging photographs into quilt-like patterns are ways to get to know your photos and the qualities you might want to emphasize or enhance. Print copies of photographs you think have potential. Print in different sizes, print in multiples, print reversals of some of the images. Cut them up, and make paper collages out of them. Being able to print your own photos in this way is a very powerful design tool.

This is a time to work on and sort ideas. Play with contrasts and similarities, keeping in mind how the visual texture appears. Look for appropriate value contrasts, color schemes, scale of images to overall size of composition, and proportion. Look also for sections of a photo that you want to crop and enlarge, often greatly enlarge. While you are handling the paper versions, you can see the different alternatives. Some of these studies will result in quilts, many will not. The activity is useful in refining your design skills, whether they become quilts or not.

DESIGN

There are many useful design principles listed in art books: rhythm, balance, unity, and so on. I have found the three that were taught to me by my friend, mentor, and art professor, Helen B. Davis, to be very useful and simple to remember: **Simplify, Exaggerate, and Repeat**. Keep in mind these three design guidelines at all stages of the design process. Simplify your images. Simpler is usually better. Exaggerate some feature of the photographed subject. Or exaggerate the perspective. Or exaggerate the contrast. Repeat images, repeat colors, repeat similar lines. These simple principles can be applied in many ways.

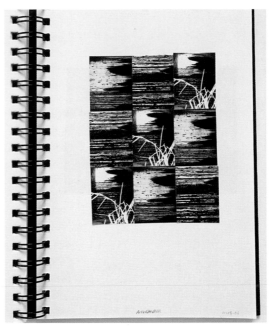

Grass/water montage: Simplify, Exaggerate, Repeat

Sky—Color Gradations

"The sky is the source of light in Nature and it governs everything." —John Constable

Many painters have spent their lives painting the sky in all its variations. The sky is available to all of us, no matter where we live. Sunsets, of course, make beautiful inspiration and can be the source of color gradations used in digital work. Cloud shapes are endlessly varied and provoke a sense of mystery and wonder for most people.

Golden skies montage

Flowers—the Most Colorful Forms

Often the most colorful objects in any environment, flowers prove irresistible to most photographers. I have far more pictures of flowers than I will ever use in my quilt work, I suspect. Still, I keep photographing the flowers in my garden, in other people's gardens, in public gardens, and of course, the wildflowers.

Falling poppies montage

Birds—Life in the Trees

Many artists find animal subjects inspirational. Birds appear in many of my quilts. They often have symbolic value in artwork, but they can be interesting simply as the life among the tree branches and amid the water images.

Bosque del Apache Wildlife Refuge montage

Trees—Branches as Lines Drawn against the Sky

Bare branches do not necessarily have a forlorn nature or symbolize the end of life. The beauty of the lines, the negative spaces carved out by them, and the patterns characteristic of different tree species are inspiring. Artists respond to and use those lines drawn by nature.

Tree branch and blue skies montage study #1

Blue Skies/Abandon, 38″ × 50″, 2006

keeping track of ideas

Keeping your photos and your digital alterations categorized by theme will help you generate ideas. There are many ways to keep track of and develop ideas. Journals and notebooks can become artwork in themselves. Find the way of keeping your visual ideas together that appeals to you. If it is something you enjoy doing, you will get more benefit out of it.

WAYS TO ORGANIZE VISUAL IDEAS

These suggestions also help to generate new ideas.

☐ Chronological photo albums arranged by date and subject—on or off the computer.

☐ Category folders of favorite photographs—on or off the computer.

☐ Photo journals where you play with photo montage and make quilt-like compositions with selected photographs—off the computer.

☐ Software-play folders, labeled by working title or subject—on the computer.

☐ Design journal with larger printed images and selected multiple quilt ideas from the design play on the computer, printed out so you can compare them. This journal also might have drawings, lists, and other pictures of things you think would contribute to your artwork—off the computer.

Photo Montage Journal as Study for Quilt Design

Materials

■ Multiple small prints of your photos in various sizes

■ Bound notebook or journal—at least 50 pages

■ Rotary cutter and ruler, or paper cutter

■ Glue stick or double-sided tape

■ Old phone book pages as a protective surface for gluing
(After running the glue off the edges of the back of the photo,
throw the phone book page away.)

■ Brayer for smoothing out the glued photos

> **TIP**
>
> I like spiral-bound notebooks because they open flat and
> expand to hold the additional paper that is added in the
> collage-montage process.

Preparation

1. Divide the notebook into 12 sections.

2. After each month has passed, select photographs that
you took during that month. Select some to crop and enlarge
details. Print several different sizes of the selected photos and
crops. Print multiples of some of them. I like to print selected
photos in multiples of 2, 3, and 5 when I'm printing them small

> **TIP**
>
> With several photos open in Photoshop Elements Editor
> mode, use the *Print Multiple Photos* option at the bottom of
> the *File* menu. This selection opens the *Photo Organizer* por-
> tion of the software. Then select *Picture Package* under *Type
> of Print* and select the *Layout* you would like to use to print a
> page of the same photo in different sizes or several different
> photos in different sizes.

3. Cut up your printed photos with a rotary cutter, clear
ruler, and cutting mat, or with scissors for less formal, non-
straight lines. If you prefer, a bolder approach would be to tear
prints freely.

Collage the Photos

Use one or all of the following ideas:

■ Make a montage of the small photographs using just the
photographs. Use any adhering method you like. I have used
both glue sticks and double-sided tape.

■ Make a collage adding colored paper strips, fabrics, or backgrounds behind the photographs.

■ Print large photographs, and cut them into different-sized
pieces. Then rearrange the parts into a collage.

If you don't like the monthly divisions, choose themes to
photograph: the seasons, gardens, everyday objects, leaves, geo-
metric shapes, colors, your travels, people, animals, or just what
you happened to have felt like taking pictures of recently.

Your journals can include a variety of montage and collage
compositions: simple ones with large images and more complicated ones with lots of images. Try to vary the sizes and the
formats. And you could add paint or colored pencil.

You can do this exercise on the computer as well. I have used
both design methods, but I like the hands-on aspect of cutting and pasting the physical pieces of paper. It feels like there
is more opportunity for improvisation and serendipity when
physically handling and moving around the images. I notice
details and design principles in the photos when I repeat images
or enlarge images. Maybe it dates back to my childhood, when
I loved cutting out paper dolls. Maybe it is more like play than
like work and frees some latent creativity in me.

techniques for printing on cloth

printers

Many different kinds of ink and printer combinations are available to us as artists, from standard inkjet printers to dye sublimation printers and printers with fiber reactive dyes in them. Doubtless, technological advances will provide us with even more options in the near future. There are businesses that will do large-format printing for you. Doing your own printing has many advantages, both for printing photos on paper and for printing your digital compositions on cloth. You can be more experimental when you do your own printing. If you make a print that isn't quite right, you can easily make adjustments and print another one. The prints you do yourself feel less precious and can be cut up, experimented with, or embellished with other art media with less inhibition because you know you can always print more.

dye-based ink or pigment ink

You can print on fabric with almost any inkjet printer, but a photo-quality printer will give you the best results. Most inkjet printers use a dye-based ink, which is not very lightfast or permanent, although pretreatment methods like using Bubble Jet Set 2000 help protect from fading and washing, as do some post-treatment methods (see page 41). I have used both a desktop inkjet printer with dye-based inks and Bubble Jet Set 2000 pretreatment, and more recently, a printer that uses pigment ink that doesn't require pretreated fabric.

Pigment inks are much more lightfast but are said to abrade more easily. However, in my tests I have **not** found them easy to scratch or rub off, wet or dry. For prints that aren't going to get a lot of washing or rubbing, the pigment ink prints are excellent. In addition, pigment inks do not need any pretreatment of the cloth. You can print directly on any fabric you can get to go through your printer. You can learn more about the character-istics of the two kinds of ink by reading Jerome's comments on the C. Jenkins website (see Resources, on page 94).

Printers come in many different sizes. The pigment ink printer I have been using most recently is an Epson Stylus Photo 2200, which will print 13 inches wide and 44 inches long. Although it is tempting to think about getting an even larger format printer, as a quilter, small units are a familiar and stimulating design element. If you want to print longer pieces of fabric, find software such as The Print Shop by Broderbund (see Resources, page 94) that will do what is usually referred to as "banner printing."

I recommend that you use the ink cartridges from the printer manufacturers. Don't substitute cheap, refilled ink cartridges, because you want the quality of a good ink, just as you want high-quality acrylic paints or fabric dyes for your artwork. The biggest danger to artwork is deterioration from light and pollution, so start with the best-quality materials.

If you are buying a printer specifically for printing on fabric, select one that is designed for printing photographs. Whether they use dye-based or pigment inks, they usually print more ink per area than other printers. If you don't know what kind of ink your printer uses, consult the user manual that came with it or check online at the manufacturer's website.

CHARACTERISTICS OF PIGMENT INK

- It is more lightfast.

- It doesn't need any pretreatment of the fabric.

- It sits on the surface rather than soaking into the fabric.

- It needs to dry longer before handling when printed on fabric—especially on rough-textured fabrics like silk noil and canvas.

techniques for printing on fabric

PREPARING THE FABRIC

If you are using a dye-based inkjet printer, pretreat your fabric with Bubble Jet Set 2000 or use pretreated fabric sheets (see Resources, on page 94). If you are using a pigment ink printer, simply iron your fabric. If you are using any of the commercially available pretreated fabrics, be sure to follow the directions on the package. I don't use pretreated fabrics, because I use a pigment ink printer and I like to print different sizes with a wide variety of fabrics. The commercially available pretreated fabrics can become expensive if you do a lot of printing on fabric.

STABILIZING THE FABRIC

Freezer paper ironed onto the back of fabric is the easiest method for stabilizing cloth to go through a printer, but many other adhesive systems will work. Lay the previously ironed fabric facedown on your ironing surface. Place the freezer paper, shiny, plastic-coated side down on top of the fabric. Iron without steam, using a moderately hot setting. Make sure there are no bubbles or wrinkles in the fabric. If the paper doesn't stick well, raise the temperature of your iron. If the freezer paper is larger than your fabric, you will be peeling it off the ironing surface. Since it doesn't leave any residue, this is not a problem.

Cut the freezer paper as you need it. It is reusable and can be used until it gets wrinkles, creases, or damaged edges or until the fabric won't stick anymore. A good place to store the cut freezer paper, labeled by size, is under a large cutting mat on your cutting table. The freezer paper does not need to be the same size as the fabric. You just have to take the margins into account when you tell the printer what size to print. (With my printers, this is the *User Defined* option. You might also see the margin data input located under the *File>Print>Page Setup* option of the software.) Extraneous threads should be trimmed. If you are using pigment inks, let the printed cloth dry overnight before removing it from the freezer paper. Some fabrics, like silk noil, are still very damp to the touch immediately after printing.

The limit on how thick your fabric can be is determined by what your printer can feed through its feed mechanism. For example, the straight-through manual feed slot on the Epson 2200 accommodates up to .05 inch, allowing many media choices, such as layered fused cloth or laminated paper-fabric combinations. Some printers allow even thicker media. Check your printer manual to see if it has adjustments for envelopes or card stock. I get less smudging if I select the *Envelope* setting on my printers.

STABILIZING WITH FREEZER PAPER

When using freezer paper to stabilize fabric for printing, remember the following:

- Freezer paper is reusable. Use it until it gets damaged, or the fabric won't stick anymore.

- Label the sheets of freezer paper on the back, according to size.

- Freezer paper sheets can be larger than the cloth rectangles.

- Store used freezer paper under your large cutting mat to keep it flat.

TROUBLESHOOTING

Try the following when feeding the fabric/freezer paper sandwich through the printer:

- Make sure the edges are straight, perpendicular, and very even on the sides—some printers are fussier about the sides than the leading edge.

- Clipping the corners of the leading edge of the freezer paper at a 45° angle can help prevent jams, especially if the paper/fabric combo tends to curl.

- You can add a strip of masking tape to the back side of the leading edge along the entire edge.

- If the fabric tends to separate from the backing, wrap masking tape from the back to the front.

- If your printer has a thickness setting, be sure to try it. Many printers have a lever to adjust for using card stock or envelopes. Check your printer manual.

BETTER PRINTS ON CLOTH

When your printer's dialogue box comes up before printing, always make sure that the options for *Best Photo* and *Photo Enhance* (or equivalent) are checked. (These options may be located under the *Printer Preferences* command.) Experiment with the different kinds of paper settings, although usually the *Plain* paper option is the best one for printing on most fabrics. You might think fabric is more like a matte-surfaced paper, but the matte setting often produces a lighter print.

A frequent mistake when printing larger than 8½ × 11 inches is not resetting the paper size to *User Defined* and then to the appropriate paper size. It is a good habit to use the *Print Preview* setting, if available. It catches lots of mistakes before they get printed.

PRINTING ON CLOTH

For best results when printing on cloth, remember the following:

☐ Always use *Best Photo, Photo Enhance,* or equivalent options in your printer's dialog box.

☐ The *Plain* paper setting works well for most fabrics.

☐ Turn off the high-speed printing option if your printer has one.

☐ Be sure to change the size of paper in the *User Defined* setting in the size menu if you are using a fabric/freezer paper sandwich larger or smaller than 8½″ × 11″.

☐ Set your thickness setting to the *Envelope* (or equivalent) setting.

☐ Use the *Print Preview* consistently to make sure the size is set correctly.

☐ In dry climates printer nozzles may dry out after prolonged nonuse, and you may have to run the nozzle cleaning mechanism several times to get all colors to print well.

ATTITUDE OF EXPERIMENTATION

It is extremely valuable to have an attitude of experimentation when printing on cloth. Be ready for mistakes—printed fabric that didn't work out, is too small or too large, has smudges or streaks, or was printed with one of the printer nozzles clogged. You should be ready for these frustrations.

An image printed on cloth is never the same as it is on paper, and because each kind of fabric takes the ink a little differently, you should make test prints on the kind of fabric you will be using. If adjustments need to be made, you can make them to the image and print again. Seeing the actual 6-inch or 12-inch printout on the design wall is often the best way to judge what size and intensity of image you want. The monitor can be deceiving.

Printed cloth mistakes are good for improvisational collage quilts because there is usually a portion of the print that is good enough to cut out and use. Mistakes can also be salvaged by additions of paint or an appliqué of other fabric images.

You can use large pieces that didn't print the way you wanted as a canvas for experimenting with painting with acrylics or using other art media over some or all of the print.

Red Fence, 8″ × 11″, 2006. A mini-quilt improvised from printed leftovers

Experiment with printing at different resolutions. Because you may not usually want photographic realism, lower resolutions often yield nice prints. When you have greatly enlarged a design, the resulting pixelation of the image gives a mottled, almost painted look (see page 49).

types of fabric

You can print on any fabric, but smooth, tightly woven and very white fabrics yield the best color and clearest prints. Experiment with all kinds of fabrics. You might discover some interesting effects. Every fabric takes the print and the color intensity differently. The tightness of the weave makes a large difference in how the print will appear. None of the prints on fabrics will look the same as prints on paper. Pima cotton and many silks give the brightest colors and the sharpest definition. Interesting contrasts in texture and fabric weave are appealing, so try silk noil, canvas, and other kinds of textured fabrics. Jacquard silks with a subtle pattern add another layer of background image under a digital print.

Detail from *Migration Dream #1* (full quilt shown on page 84). Notice contrast of cotton (on right) and silk noil (on left).

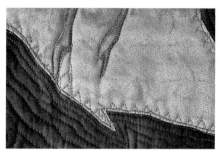

Printing on jacquard silk

Different background tones can drastically affect the colors on the print. Slightly off-white or yellowish tones will cause either graying or warming of the colors. You will learn gradually what needs to be done to the fabrics you are using to achieve your desired effect.

Splendid Moment, 42″ × 28″, 2003

basic photo editing for fabric printing

You rarely get a good print on cloth without making any adjustments to the image on your computer with your photo-editing software. Your results will be faint and very disappointing unless you enhance your photo with some or all of the following methods. Every photo will need different treatment for the effect you want.

RESIZING, RESOLUTION, AND RESAMPLING

You most likely will want to change the sizes of your images as you are working with them. In Photoshop Elements, look for resizing in the *Image>Resize>Image Size* drop-down menu. If you've never used this feature, consult the online help for resizing in your photo-editing software. More help with resizing, resampling, and resolution can be found on the C&T website in Photoshop Elements Basics (www.ctpub.com) and by using the Photoshop Elements drop-down *Help* menu.

Resolution determines the quality of your printed image and is measured in ppi (pixels per inch) on your computer and in dpi (dots per inch) on the printer.

As you make an image larger, the resolution automatically is reduced if you don't have the *Resample* box checked. While resolutions of around 300 ppi are considered optimal for printing realistic photographs on paper, a photo with a resolution as low as 72 ppi can print nicely on fabric **if** you are altering the photo and it does not need to have clear and realistic details. If you want to maintain a higher resolution when enlarging a photo, check the *Resample* box (which either adds or subtracts pixels from your image). While resampling can result in a so-called "degraded image," this may not matter for painterly designs. You can improve the image by using the *Unsharp Mask* filter afterward (page 39).

The **optimum ppi** for printing depends on the kind of image you want and on the cloth you are printing on. For example, prints on thin habotai silks will bleed at the color edges a little anyway, so a low resolution of 72 ppi does not make much difference. Remember, if most of these images are incorporated into a large quilt, they will be seen from a distance, and details and edges may not be as important. For my purposes, I don't think there is any reason to go much over 300 ppi.

> **TIP**
> When resizing and resampling an image to make it bigger, select *Bicubic Smoother* from the *Resample Image* drop-down menu. When making an image smaller, use *Bicubic Sharper*.

EXERCISE 4 *Resolution*

Select a photo and print it in a variety of sizes and resolutions using different fabrics to see the differences. Label all your samples for future reference.

ENHANCE SATURATION

Fabric is more absorbent than paper, so you generally need to enhance saturation quite a bit to get a good printed image. In Photoshop Elements, select *Enhance>Adjust Color>Adjust Hue/Saturation.* Increase the *Saturation* +20 to +30 on the slider for master color saturation editing. You often will want to adjust the saturation for one or more individual colors as well. From the *Edit* box in *Hue/Saturation* (*Enhance>Adjust Color>Adjust Hue/Saturation>Edit*), select the specific color you want to adjust. The resulting colors will look somewhat garish on your monitor screen but will print satisfactorily on the cloth.

ENHANCE CONTRAST

For a desirable printed image, you most likely will also need to increase the contrast. In Photoshop Elements, select *Enhance>Adjust Lighting>Brightness/Contrast.* Increase the *Contrast* by +20 to +30 on the slider to get a good image. Sometimes making the image a little darker results in a better print. A negative number on the *Brightness* slider makes the whole image darker and deeper in color if tweaked just a little.

SHARPENING

Most prints on cloth will also be improved if the image is sharpened. The sharpening filters increase the contrast of adjacent pixels. To sharpen the image you can use any of the three sharpening filters, but using the *Unsharp Mask* (yes, that is really what it is called) filter is usually preferred. Click on *Enhance>Unsharp Mask* and experiment with the three sliders (*Amount*, *Radius*, and *Threshold*). Check the *Preview* button on and off to see the effect of the changes on your image. *Amount* refers to the intensity of the effect or "sharpness" you add to the edges of objects, *Radius* controls how many pixels around each sample will be affected, and *Threshold* governs how much difference between pixels is needed to determine an edge. (A setting of 0 affects every edge and settings over 50 affect very few pixels.) You will need to experiment by printing a test on the fabric you think you will be using. An excellent explanation of this can be found in Gloria Hansen's *Digital Essentials* (see Resources, page 94).

> **TIP**
>
> In early versions of Photoshop Elements, *Unsharp Mask* is in the *Filter* drop-down menu: *Filter>Sharpen>Unsharp Mask*. In later versions of Photoshop Elements, click on *Enhance>Unsharp Mask*.

OVERLAY BLENDING OF TWO LAYER COPIES

Using the *Overlay blending* mode with two identical layers also results in a deeper and more contrasting print. (Refer to page 58 for more about using blending modes with layers.)

BLACKS

If your printer has the option of different black ink cartridges, try them instead of the standard black ink cartridge. The matte black cartridge that is an option with my pigment ink printer usually gives a more intense black on cloth prints than the photo black cartridge. However, it still is not as intense as a dyed or painted black. Black may need to be enhanced with colored pencil, acrylic paint, or appliquéd dyed or painted fabrics to achieve the desired intensity and darkness of value. Or, if a very intense black is necessary to your design, try one of the precoating products such as inkAID or Golden Digital Grounds (page 41; and Resources, page 94).

Original photo as it appears on the screen, with no adjustments

Photo with enhanced hue saturation (+30)

Photo with both enhanced hue saturation and sharpening with the *Unsharp Mask* filter

DOUBLE PRINTS

Another way to intensify the color in a fabric print is to run the cloth through twice (waiting overnight for the first ink to dry) with the same image and exactly the same settings. You risk a slight offset and blurring of edges, but it does give a very intense color when it works.

printing on hand-dyed or painted cloth

Printing on hand-dyed fabrics works quite well. You have to keep in mind that the dyed colors will affect your printed ink colors. There are interesting possibilities for printing an image in the light areas of a hand-dyed fabric.

To some extent, acrylic paints on fabrics, especially the metallics, function as a resist, so the fabric doesn't always take the ink very well. However, different paints and various dilutions seem to operate differently, and I have gotten some very interesting effects by just experimenting (see my quilt *Migration Dream #2* on page 87). For printing over extensively painted surfaces, you may want to try the precoatings discussed on the following page.

Bird print on dyed fabric at left and on white sponged acrylic on black at right in *Blue Bird*, 8˝ × 11˝, 2006

inkAID and golden digital grounds

For the most vivid color and a paint-like surface, try using inkAID (see Resources, page 94). It is a coating you paint on the paper or cloth before you print to achieve the vivid colors similar to photographic paper. It does **drastically** change the "hand" and look of the cloth, making it quite stiff. This stiffness makes it good for doing machine embroidery but not as good for hand embroidery. Golden, a maker of acrylic paints, also has several digital ground media for painting on papers, fabrics, and other surfaces that make the printer inks look like the prints achieved on special photographic papers (see Resources, page 94). Both inkAID and Golden Digital Grounds come in an opaque finish for strong colors and direct printing and also a transparent or gloss finish for printing over previously painted surfaces.

For the quilts *Red Maple Symmetry, Saffron Symmetry* (page 9), and *Return of the Robins* (page 49), I used inkAID as a pretreatment before printing on some or all of the fabrics.

Original maple leaf photo

Color-changed maple leaf photo

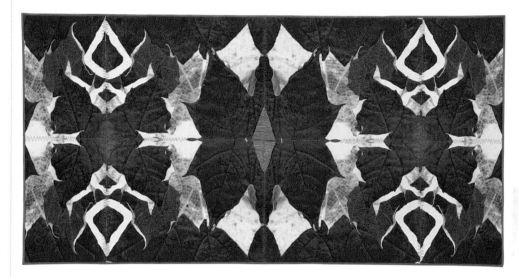
Printed using inkAID painted on cotton, *Red Maple Symmetry,* 43˝ × 22˝, 2005

Detail from *Red Maple Symmetry*

post treatments

There are many options for a final protection treatment. One option is to spray with UV-Resistant Clear Acrylic Coating made by Krylon (see Resources, page 94). It comes in both glossy and matte finishes. This mainly adds some UV protection for the fabric prints, but it **also causes a slight enhancement of the colors** and a slight stiffening of the surface. Krylon also makes a product called Preserve It! This product is made for protecting digital photos on paper and other surfaces from UV light and moisture changes. Alternatively, you can add a layer of protection and enhance the colors by painting with matte or glossy acrylic medium, or a varnish with UV protection. This creates a paint-like surface. (Golden makes several such products, including a spray varnish with UVL protection; see Resources, page 94.) Use the mediums, not the varnishes, if you are adding further paint to the image. Varnishes are intended to be the last layer on your artwork and are for final protection. Test these on sample prints before using them on your quilts, but I have used these with both pigment ink and dye-based ink prints on my quilts. Any of these products can be used to add a final layer of protection against fading, moisture, or air pollutants.

simple ways to use printed photographs

Many photographs can be used for printing on cloth with very little image altering, beyond the enhancement techniques described in Chapter 4 (starting on page 34). Other photographs need editing to eliminate unwanted backgrounds or distracting elements.

minimally altered photos

Some images can be resized to different proportions without sacrificing realism. *After the Storm II: Thoughts about Mahler* (facing page) is a quilt which started from four pictures that were not altered but were made into a panorama, stitched together by the software from the camera. (Photoshop Elements also has this feature, as do many cameras. In Photoshop Elements, click *File > New > Photomerge Panorama*.) The images were then altered by stretching the whole picture both vertically and horizontally. The panorama was made to a 29 × 12-inch size, resampled, and printed at a resolution of 180 ppi onto pima cotton. (In this case resampling meant that some pixels were added to make the image larger. See page 38 for more information.) It is interesting that the sky still looks very realistic, even though the alteration distorted it. Smaller repeats of the panorama were used on the top edge of the quilt. Additional photos of sky and trees in window reflections were added to the bottom edge of the quilt. The middle section was composed of hand-dyed fabrics as well as some leftover printed fabric from a previous quilt.

Original sky photos taken in panorama mode

Resulting panorama automatically stitched together by camera software

Altered panorama for printing 29″ × 12″

Detail of *After the Storm II: Thoughts about Mahler*

After the Storm II: Thoughts about Mahler, 29″ × 24″, 2006

slightly altered photographs

Slightly altered photographs can be useful in traditional piecing designs as well as collaged designs. Crop sections of photographs (click on the *Crop Tool* in the *Toolbox* on the left side of the screen), enlarge them (*Image>Resize>Image Size*), print them on fabric, and cut them into squares, triangles, or strips for use in piecing. *Mill Creek Aspen Forest #1* (see facing page) was created with fused appliqué, loosely mimicking traditional log cabin piecing. My scanned photos were printed, cut into strips, and combined with dyed and silk-screened fabrics and a print from a scanned leaf skeleton. The print color was exaggeratedly enhanced (page 38) to a brighter, more yellowish tone. Several enlarged and cropped sizes were used to print on 8½ × 11-inch sheets of pima cotton. The prints were cut into strips of varying widths to use in the log cabin-style arrangement.

Scanned leaf skeleton, color altered, cropped, and enlarged

Cropped and color-altered image

Cropped again and enlarged image for print

Cropped again and further enlarged image for print

Mill Creek Aspen Forest #1, 44″ × 24″, 2002

Details of *Mill Creek Aspen Forest #1*

tiling

TILED PHOTOGRAPHS (POSTER PRINTING)

Most printers have the option of printing tiled photos. This option is found in the dialogue box that comes up when you send a photo to be printed. It may be in the *Page Layout* section and is usually called *Poster Printing*. One alternative location is the *Print>Printer Properties>Output>Output Mode* section. This function divides a picture into a regular number of 8½ × 11-inch pages, or tiles. You have the option of printing with edges (for seam allowances) or not, and the option of how many tiles (usually four, nine, or sixteen; some desktop publishing software enables even more tiles). *Blue Sky Aspen Forest Window* was created from one photograph of aspen trees taken looking up toward the sky. Four page-size tiles were printed from this one photograph, and each page was cut into four rectangles. Then lattice strips were fused between the sixteen parts of the picture to make the quilt top.

Blue Sky Aspen Forest Window, 21˝ × 29˝, 2002

Original photo

Self-Selected Tiles

You can also divide a larger digital composition into separate rectangles, each a different size, and print them on separate pieces of fabric. Two of the quilts in the *My Favorite Tree* series, *Basking in the Sun* (page 48) and *Quaking in the Wind* (page 53), use this technique. After altering a photo for color (page 62) and simplifying it with the *Cutout filter* (page 52), I greatly enlarged my design, resizing (page 38) the image to the 40 × 60-inch approximate size of the intended quilt. The resolution of the image was 72 ppi, but it printed well even at this low resolution. I divided the whole design into nine sections as follows. Using the **Crop Tool** (in the **Toolbox** on the left side of the screen), I cropped each piece into a printable size and saved each of the nine different rectangles so they could be printed as separate image files. The photo at lower right shows the nine printed sections overlaid on a black background, creating the effect of thick black lines between the sections. For additional information on this process, see C&T Publishing's website for Photoshop Elements Basics (www.ctpub.com).

I altered each of the nine rectangles in slightly different ways. Some were made larger and cropped in relation to the other parts, some were made brighter, some were made darker, some were made lighter, some were printed on previously dyed yellow fabric. I assembled the pieces in collage fashion, with the overlapped raw edges accentuated by a free-motion zigzag stitching. I added metallic foiling before quilting.

TIP

Always save a copy of your original design in addition to the one you are working with. Also save each individual rectangle printed in case you need to reprint it.

My favorite tree original photo

My favorite tree with *Cutout filter* applied (page 52)

My favorite tree, color-altered (page 62)

My favorite tree showing sections to be printed

Basking in the Sun, 34″ × 42″, 2003

Detail showing foil on tree trunk

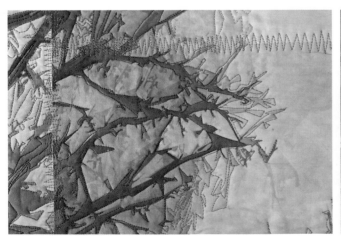

Detail showing portion of quilt printed on dyed yellow fabric

Detail showing stitched edges of section

enlarged backgrounds

If your printer can print long sizes or you are using software that prints long banner sizes (page 34), you can break up your quilt design into three, four, or more long strips such as 8½″ × 36″ or 13″ × 44″. One large picture divided up this way provided the background for *Return of the Robins,* below. This sunset photo was enhanced for *Brightness* and *Saturation* (page 38). Then I enlarged it to 36″ × 60″, a little larger than the estimated size for the finished quilt. This made the resolution low and the image quite pixelated and grainy, but also more atmospheric. I divided the enlarged image into five strips and printed each individually. The widest strip that my printer can accommodate is 13″, so that is how I determined where to crop the image. I printed each strip at 13″ × 36″ and further trimmed a few in the assembly process. When reassembled, the printed strips served as the background for the quilt. Smaller rectangles of robins, sky, branches, and so on were appliquéd on top. Many of the smaller insets used smaller versions of the sky and mountain backdrop, adding repeated visual elements. The brighter images were printed on an inkAID-coated cotton surface (page 41). The entire finished quilt was coated with a matte acrylic varnish to further brighten the colors.

Background divided into five strips 13″ × 36″

Enhanced photo background used in *Return of the Robins*

One of the additional prints used

Return of the Robins, 34″ × 55″, 2006

You can have a different design in each strip of your background image. *Birds in the Bush* (page 76) has multiple background sections and a large tree digitally layered over several of the background pieces, with added silk rectangles of birds appliquéd onto the background. These are the same robins used in *Return of the Robins* (page 49). (For more discussion of the robin color variations, see pages 69–70.)

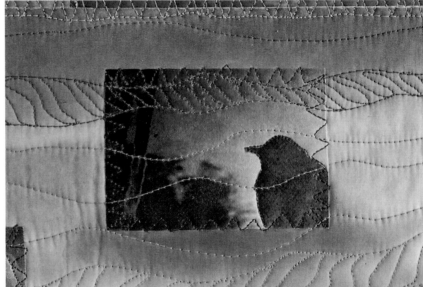

Details of *Return of the Robins*

simple editing, selecting, and erasing

The Photoshop Elements tools and techniques described below will give you many options for eliminating unwanted elements when you are altering images.

The techniques encompass using the various *Selection tools* including the *Lasso Tool*, *Magic Wand Tool*, *Clone Stamp Tool,* and *Crop Tool,* and using the *Eraser Tool* (all found in the *Toolbox* on the left side of the screen) combined with a *Delete* option. It's best to try them out, and, as needed, click the *Help* drop-down menu with your software, check your software's online help, or see the C&T Photoshop Elements Basics (www.ctpub.com) for help using them.

These techniques take some practice to use skillfully; however shortcuts often produce interesting results. For example, selecting only the branches of a tree image could be time-consuming and tricky. It is much easier to use the *Lasso Tool* (in newer versions of Photoshop Elements, three *Lasso tools* are available when you click on the triangle at the bottom of the visible *Lasso Tool* command) or the *Magic Wand Tool* for selecting, and include the background between branches and around the edges of the tree in your selection. This gives interesting effects when the images are layered (pages 57–59), as can be seen in many of the tree images I have used.

Trees selected with some background included (See pages 74, 78, and 80 to see various uses of these tree branches.)

Original tree photo

Erasing unwanted parts of a photograph is often easier if you use the *Clone Stamp Tool.* It replaces the unwanted area with pixels like the ones to the side of your unwanted area.

You can remove part of an image by using the *Crop Tool.* Your drop-down *Help* section will show all the choices. By left-clicking with your mouse, you can drag a rectangle beyond which everything will be eliminated.

The *Eraser Tool* changes pixels in an image when you drag through them. If you are working on a background layer, the erased pixels change to the background color; otherwise, they become transparent. There are options for different sizes and kinds of brushes and for the opacity of your erasing. Check your drop-down *Help* command, and practice using this tool.

Learning to use the *Copy* and *Paste* commands will be a big help when playing with altering your photos. These commands are found in the drop-down *Edit* menu. You must first select an area to be copied, using one of the *Selection tools,* or choose *Select All* from the *Selection* drop-down menu to select the whole picture. After selecting and copying, you can *Paste* into your image as many copies as you want of the selected area.

EXERCISE 5
Editing Practice

> **TIP**
>
> To open multiple photos at once on your screen, click *File>Open,* and find your first photo. Repeat with additional photos. Then click *Window>Images>Tile* to view all your photos at once. You may need to resize or move images by clicking on the corner to fit them on your screen.

■ Practice using the various selection tools to select a part of one photograph and *Copy* and *Paste* it into another photograph. Practice enlarging or distorting the selection and pasting the different selections into your composition.

■ Practice using the *Clone Stamp Tool* to get rid of unwanted blemishes or lines. This tool is also useful for enlarging areas of color.

■ Practice using the *Eraser* tools on some of your photographs or digital creations. (One of three eraser tools will be visible in the *Toolbox*; right-click in the bottom right corner of the eraser to access them.) Investigate the *Background Eraser Tool,* which allows you to erase backgrounds at the edges of high-contrast objects.

beyond photographs

simplifying images to make them more graphic

When you start thinking beyond printing realistic photographs, you start thinking of ways to change the imagery. You want to make your own unique designs, to create a particular mood or style, and to reduce detail. These are times when you don't want your images to look like photographs printed on fabric. You want them to look like paintings, drawings, or silk-screen prints. To accomplish this, generally you want to simplify your images.

You can use various filters to simplify your photographic images and make them look less photographically realistic. The standard software filters can look pretty predictable, but with careful use, they can transform a photo into an appealing design. Although you may be using the *Artistic filters*, your aim is not to mimic other artistic media as much as to reduce a lot of the photographic detail that tells our brain that it is a realistic photograph. Thus the images become more painterly and more graphic, as if produced some other way.

> **TIP**
> Try some of the Photoshop Elements *Enhance>Auto Smart Fix, Auto Levels,* or *Auto Contrast* tools on your photos **both before and after** applying filters. They sometimes dramatically change a design.

CUTOUT FILTER

One of my favorite filters for simplifying images is called *Cutout (Filter>Artistic>Cutout)*. It is designed to make an image look as though it were cut out of layers of colored papers. It combines similar pixels into larger forms and reduces the number of values and colors. You have a great deal of control over the amount of these changes. You can reduce the number of colors or tones, and you can vary the way the filter simplifies the edges. Three adjustment sliders control different amounts of alteration: *Number of Levels, Edge Simplicity,* and *Edge Fidelity.* Used in combination, these sliders create a variety of effects. The original image used in the *My Favorite Tree Series* is shown varied three ways, changing only the *Edge Simplicity* slider. Each *Cutout filter* was applied individually to the original photo.

Original photo before *Cutout filter* applied

Cutout filter **applied,** *Number of Levels* **= 8,** *Edge Simplicity* **= 6,** *Edge Fidelity* **= 1**

Cutout filter **applied,** *Number of Levels* **= 8,** *Edge Simplicity* **= 4,** *Edge Fidelity* **= 1**

Cutout filter **applied,** *Number of Levels* **= 8,** *Edge Simplicity* **= 8,** *Edge Fidelity* **= 1**

For *Quaking in the Wind*, I used the *Cutout filter* to give the tree an otherworldly, unrealistic look, sort of bent and broken. This image also was divided into sections to be altered, printed separately, and ultimately sewn together (see page 47).

A print used in *Quaking in the Wind*

Quaking in the Wind, 34″ × 42″, 2003

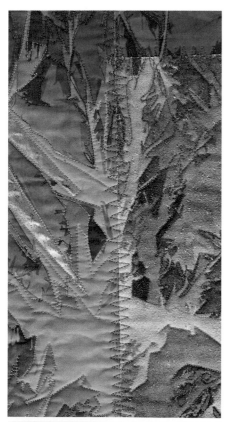

Notice contrast of silk noil on right, cotton prints, and foiling

DRY BRUSH AND WATERCOLOR FILTERS

The *Dry Brush filter* (*Filter>Artistic>Dry Brush*) simplifies a photographic image by reducing the range of colors, thus eliminating much realistic detail. There are three adjustment sliders: *Brush Size*, *Brush Detail*, and *Texture*. As with any of the filters, you need to play with the adjustment sliders to see what differences they make in combination with each other. The *Watercolor filter* (*Filter>Artistic>Watercolor*) also creates an interesting simplification. This filter saturates the colors at the edges, mimicking some watercolor painting effects, and also has the ability to accentuate shadows nicely. Using the *Unsharp Mask* (page 39) after applying a filter often accentuates the changes. Some of the effects will be more noticeable when the image is cropped and enlarged. Compare the following photos to see the effect of each filter applied individually to the original photo.

Original photo

Dry Brush filter applied; *Brush Size* = 10, *Brush Detail* = 0, *Texture* = 3; sharpened

Watercolor filter applied, *Brush Detail* = 2, *Shadow Intensity* = 1, *Texture* = 3

Cropped and further enlarged after *Dry Brush filter* applied

HINTS FOR USING FILTERS

☐ Using more than one filter on the same image eliminates the telltale canned filter look.

☐ The effects of the filters are more noticeable on lower-resolution images.

☐ Enlarged details from a photo show the effects dramatically.

☐ Using the same filter in successive applications compounds the effects.

☐ For some photos, increasing the brightness or contrast values before applying the filter will heighten the effect.

simple ways of changing colors

Changing color is one of the most engrossing things to do with images using image-editing software. You really feel like one of the gods on Mount Olympus when you start playing with color changes. The various software programs provide multiple ways to do this. With today's computers and printers, we can create millions of colors.

ENHANCE/CHANGE HUE

The simplest way to change color is to use the *Enhance>Adjust Color>Adjust Hue/Saturation* drop-down menu, which gives you three sliders to play with: *Hue, Saturation,* and *Lightness.* The *Hue* slider can be used to greatly or subtly alter the entire color spectrum in your photo, or you can select one of the six color families to adjust either subtly or boldly. Very interesting effects can be achieved when the color changes are applied **after** an artistic filter has been used on a photographic enlargement, as shown below. In this sequence, the *Posterize filter* created more definite lines and shapes and a reduced number of colors (*Filter>Adjustments>Posterize*). Note that each filter change was applied individually to the original photo on the previous page.

Enlarged detail of Virginia creeper leaf, *Posterize filter* applied

Enlarged posterized detail with *Hue slider* set at +40

Enlarged posterized detail with *Hue slider* set at –74

Enlarged posterized detail with *Hue slider* set at +160

Lovely gradations can be achieved with a systematic change in the *Hue adjustment slider*, as shown below, where each hue adjustment was applied individually to the original photo. Individual colors can be lightened or darkened with the *Lightness slider* but if used on the entire photo, it can gray or reduce the tonal variations unpleasantly.

Original bud photo

First example hue adjustment

Second example hue adjustment

Third example hue adjustment

Fourth example hue adjustment

Fifth example hue adjustment

You can also change aspects of the color in the *Enhance>Adjust Color>Color Variations* menu, with more delicate control over *Midtones*, *Shadows*, *Highlights*, and *Saturation*. An example of the kinds of color changes using the *Midtones* option is shown below.

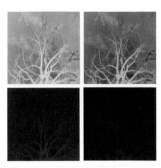

Original digital designs in four values of gray

Red added to original

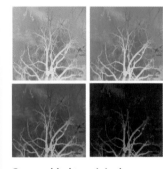

Green added to original

Yellow added to original by decreasing blue

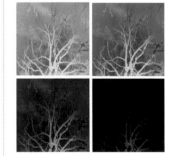

Blue added to original

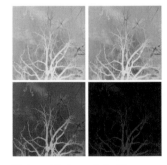

Violet added to original by decreasing green

> **TIP**
>
> For simple color tone enhancements, try the photo filters found in Photoshop Elements in the *Filter>Adjustments> Photo Filter* menu. This contains a menu of simulated camera filters that can enhance or change the entire photo or selected portions. Try some out, and see how they work on your selected photo.

PAINT BUCKET TOOL

One way to change only selected color areas is to use the *Paint Bucket Tool* located in the *Toolbox* on the left side of the screen. It is often useful for changing large areas of color. It dumps the selected color, replacing all the pixels of one original color. It can be difficult to learn to use this tool delicately, but interesting, bold, painterly effects can be achieved with practice and play. Select the *Foreground* color you want to use, then select the *Paint Bucket Tool*. Choose from the various options, including *Pattern, Opacity, Tolerance,* and *Contiguous*.

TIP

Foreground and background colors are selected using the color selection boxes at the bottom of the *Toolbox*. With the default settings, the upper left color swatch is for the foreground, the lower swatch is the background color.

The *Pattern* option lets you replace pixels with a stored pattern, like the painted circles photo pattern (below, right). There are stored patterns to select from, and you can create your own from any photograph. To create a custom pattern, make a rectangular selection with the *Feather* option set to 0 in the photo or drawing that has your desired pattern, and choose *Edit>Define Pattern* from the drop-down menu, then choose a name when the name box appears. Your pattern will now appear in the *Pattern* menu.

Opacity controls how much the original image shows through the color (or pattern) that is being poured on. Note that you set the opacity **before** you use the tool; it can't be changed after the color is poured.

Tolerance controls how selective the color replacement will be. With a low tolerance, a narrow range of pixels within a close color range will be recolored. With a high tolerance, a broader range of pixels will be recolored.

When the *Contiguous* option is **not** checked, the *Paint Bucket Tool* recolors all the pixels that match the selected pixel; when the *Contiguous* option is checked, the *Paint Bucket Tool* fills only connecting pixels.

Original cloud and tree digital composition

Cloud and tree design using *Paint Bucket Tool* to add lime green in selected cloud areas

Cloud and tree design using *Paint Bucket Tool* to add circles pattern to selected cloud areas

BRUSH TOOLS

The various *Brush Tool* options comprise a complex set of tools that have so many uses they could fill another book. However, a simple use is to wash a light color over an area to lightly affect a number of colors in that area. Other options include *Brush Presets*, *Size*, *Mode*, and *Opacity*. Try different options, and see what effects you can achieve.

Cloud layer brushed with blue at 75% opacity and a *Natural* brush style

using layers and blending modes for changing colors

Layers in an image composition are like stacked transparent sheets of glass on which you have photographic images. The blending modes provide different ways of looking through or combining the images. This is probably the most powerful property in the image-editing software world because you can combine your layers in many, many different ways to achieve a multitude of effects. Layer modifications can be accessed through the *Menu bar,* and some commands also appear in the *Layers palette* on the right side of the screen. Note that you pick the active layer in the *Layers palette* by clicking on it, and you can choose which layers are visible by clicking the eyeball to the left of the layer thumbnail on and off. The *Layer>Arrange* command in the drop-down menu allows you to reorder your layers from top to bottom, which is important when combining them as you work on your design.

BLENDING WITH A SOLID COLOR FILL

When using a photo as a background layer and then adding a color fill layer (*Layer>New Fill Layer>Solid Color*) as the first layer superimposed on the background, you can change colors in many ways. (*Color fill* layers can be opened in several ways. Look in the *Layer* drop-down menu or use *Help* to find other options.) *Blending modes* control the interaction of the layers. (Note that you must first create the layer, then the layer can be modified as you wish.) In newer versions of Photoshop

Elements, the option of *Blending modes* is found in the upper left corner of the *Layers palette* under the drop-down bar *Normal*. Each of the blending modes will produce a different effect. *Darken* or *Multiply* will add amounts of the selected hue to all parts of the photo, intensifying the image if it is a similar color, graying if it is a complementary color, and somewhere in between for other color differences. *Overlay* intensifies the added color effect but preserves some of the lighter and darker areas. The *Difference* and *Exclusion* blending modes create almost opposite colors, like in a color negative. Examples of the clouds and tree design with a blue color fill layer added over the entire photo using an *Overlay* blend and a *Difference* blend are shown below.

> **TIP**
> Different effects often happen when the color fill layer is under the photo layer rather than on top of the photo layer.

Solid blue color fill

Clouds and tree design with solid blue color fill layer as top layer using *Overlay blend*

Clouds and tree design with solid blue color fill layer as top layer using *Difference blend*

> **TIP**
> If the blending mode creates too strong an effect for your liking, adjust the *Opacity* using the slider located in the upper right corner of the *Layers* palette. You can also enter a percentage.

Blending with a Gradient Color Fill

Similar to adding a layer that blends with a solid color is adding a *Gradient color fill*, which can grade from light to dark, from transparent to opaque, or from one color to another—also top to bottom, left to right, or in circular or diamond pattern (*Layer>New Fill Layer>Gradient*). You can play with many, many possibilities here. The software comes with some preset gradations, but you can also create your own. Check the *Help* section to learn how to do this with your software.

Lavender to transparent *Gradient fill*

Clouds and tree with lavender to transparent *Gradient color fill* added on top using *Lighten blend*

Blending a Photo with Its Copy

Making a copy of a photo or digital design into a different layer and blending it with different modes can change or intensify the colors. If you use the *Overlay* or *Multiply blending modes*, the color intensifies. This is also a good way to print more intense colors (*Layer>Duplicate Layer>* then *Normal>Overlay* or *Multiply*).

Blending a Photo with Its Inverted Copy

The *Invert* feature is like making a negative of your image. It reverses colors to their opposite values and changes the colors to ones similar to their complements on a color wheel. Much like a color negative, it is somewhat unpredictable as to how the colors will change, but with continued use, you begin to learn what will happen. (The *Invert* feature is often found in the *Filter* menu, but some versions of Photoshop Elements have it under the command *Adjustments* in the *Filter* menu.) Combining the inverted photo with the original photo in different blending modes yields different color changes. An additional color blend or gradient layer can change everything as well. You can spend endless hours playing with combinations of these tools.

Original cloud and tree digital composition

Clouds and tree design using *Invert*

Clouds and tree design with *Invert* layer on top and *Difference blend*

COMBINE TWO PHOTOS WITH BLENDING MODES

A method I frequently use to change color is *Difference* blending or *Exclusion* blending using two photos, each in a different layer. This both changes the colors dramatically and also blends the two images. My quilt *Winter Window* (facing page) used this as the only color alteration for the quilt prints. In this case, it didn't matter which photo was on the top layer. After quilting, I sponged snow on with acrylic paint.

Second original photo of trees and rooftops against the sky, opened as another layer

Original photo of tree against the sky

The two photos layered together with *Exclusion blend*

Another example of how you can achieve an **intense** color change, with or without a gradient, while at the same time blending one photo with another one, is shown in these four prints from the design work for *Blue Hills* (page 72).

Second original photo with *Cutout filter* applied

Original photo of cow and barn

Winter Window, 33″ × 22″, 2007

Photos combined with *Difference blend*

Alternative version of photos combined with brown *Gradient fill* layer in between with *Multiply blend*

ATMOSPHERIC COLOR CHANGES

If the second blending photograph is something subtle, like clouds, you achieve a color change with only a vague cloud image noticeable, depending on the blending mode used. If you also add in a *Gradient color fill,* you can achieve dramatic color changes. These steps make up the digital composition used for *Basking in the Sun* (pages 47–48).

My favorite tree layered with cloud, *Difference blend*

My favorite tree before color change

Cloud photograph layer

Cloud combined with orange-purple *Gradient fill, Soft Light blend*

My favorite tree with cloud and orange-purple *Gradient fill, Difference blend*

ADDED TRADITIONAL ART MEDIA

Touch-ups are allowed! You can augment your fabric prints with traditional art media. One of my favorites for an overall color intensification or shading change is to use Prismacolor colored pencils. They are soft and work well on most fabrics. They have a slight matte texture, so you want to take this into account when you use them on reflective silks like silk charmeuse.

Permanent markers, such as Prismacolor markers (with either broad or narrow tips) or permanent Sharpies, can be used to highlight color. The Prismacolor markers come in a wide range of colors, similar to the colored pencils. *Virginia Creeper Vines* (page 91) has black permanent marker outlines defining the leaf shapes, as well as stitchery.

There are, of course, endless possibilities for enhancement with acrylic paints, both traditional and those specially designed for fabrics. Experiment on your leftover printed images.

drawing effects and filters

SKETCH

Various filters can be used to add a sketch-like image or quality to your composition. Photoshop Elements has fourteen different *Sketch filters*, all with several adjustment sliders. Illustrated here are *Photocopy*, *Charcoal*, and *Stamp.* Each turns the image into a black-and-white sketch that resembles the art technique for which it is named. Each has several sliders to adjust features such as light/dark balance, detail, charcoal thickness, or smoothness of line.

Original photo of hanging leaf

Filter>Sketch>Photocopy filter applied to hanging leaf photo

Filter>Sketch>Charcoal filter applied to hanging leaf photo

Filter>Sketch>Stamp filter applied to hanging leaf photo

Combining a sketch with an original photo can accentuate edges and details nicely, or you can add a drawing over the top of a second photo.

Combination of *Filter>Sketch>Stamp drawing* with original photo, *Multiply blend* mode

Stretched *Filter>Sketch>Stamp drawing* layered over leaf reflection photo with *Darken blend*

If you want a one-color sketch, set your background color to the color you want, leaving the foreground color at black. A two-color sketch can be made by setting both background and foreground colors (page 57) to the desired colors.

Purple and black sketch

> **TIP**
>
> An image can be stretched either by resizing (page 38) and specifically entering the desired height and width (without constraining proportions) or by using the handles on the edges of an image and using the cursor to drag an edge.

EXAGGERATING FEATURES

Another technique you can try is one that exaggerates features like outlines in a different way from drawing effects. One filter called *Glowing Edges* is found under *Filter>Stylize*. It can create additional outline effects when combined with a photo. It is often most desirable to use inverted (*Filter>Adjustments>Invert*).

Original hanging leaf

Hanging leaf with *Glowing Edges* filter

Original hanging leaf photo with *Glowing Edges* added as a layer blending with the *Difference* mode

Other *Stylize* filters, such as *Emboss,* can add even more exaggerated effects to your images, especially in combination with other filters and layers.

Hanging leaf with *Glowing Edges* filters and *inverted*

Emboss filter combined with original hanging leaf photo with *Difference* blend

EXERCISE 6 *Simplifying Filters*

Take one of your favorite photographs and transform it with at least five different artistic filters in your software. Photoshop Elements has many: *Colored Pencil, Cutout, Dry Brush, Film Grain, Fresco, Neon Glow, Paint Daubs, Palette Knife, Plastic Wrap, Poster Edges, Rough Pastels, Smudge Stick, Sponge, Underpainting,* and *Watercolor.* Other software programs have many filters also. Print labeled, similar-sized images, along with the original photo, to keep in your design notebook to remind you of the possibilities.

EXERCISE 7 *Changing Colors*

Take one of your favorite images, and play with different methods of changing its colors. Print similar-sized images and notes about adjustments to keep in your design notebook to remind you of the possibilities.

EXERCISE 8
Compare Black-and-White Sketches

Select a strong value contrast photo that you think would make a good sketch, and try at least three different sketch filters, like the *Charcoal, Stamp, Photocopy,* or *Conté Crayon.* Print similar-sized images to keep in your design notebook.

EXERCISE 9
Combine Two Photographs

Find two photographs to combine in different layers using different blending modes. And of course keep some printed copies with notes for your design notebook.

WORKING WITH LAYERS

Notice that when you create layers, all the layers for one background image show up in the *Layers palette.* If you import a second photo into the document window on your screen and click on that image, you can then create layers linked to that photo. The layers you created for the first photo still exist, but you can't see them until you click on that image on your screen.

To combine a layer from one photo file into the second, click on the desired layer of the first photo in the *Layers palette,* and drag onto the open image on your screen of the second photo. Now the fun begins!

TIP

Keep written notes on how you made the transformations. It is very helpful to have these notes at a later date, especially at the beginning of learning digital transformation techniques. It also saves time trying to re-create the effect later.

constructing
more complex images

After you have some experience with simplifying images by using filters and changing colors, you will understand how more complex images can be achieved. More complex imagery is a matter of building multiple layers with multiple blending modes and multiple filters. You also can see that one image can be varied in so many ways that it can be used to create different moods for different quilts. Several detailed examples of the changes made to simple photographs are explained below.

> **TIP**
>
> Always flatten your complex layered images before printing. This combines your visible layers with the background and decreases the file size. It will then take less computing time to complete your photo enhancements, but keep a copy of the layered, non-flattened design in case you want to make alterations to it. One path to flattening is *Layer>Flatten Image*. Consult your *Help* section for more information about flattening.

Deidre's cottonwood tree

One winter morning at sunrise, I took a picture of my neighbor's cottonwood tree, through both a window and a screen. This is not generally thought to be a good way to take a photograph. You can see the distortion even in the original photograph—the moiré effect that the screen caused is obvious. When the *Cutout filter* (page 52) was applied, it exaggerated those slight grid marks, creating interesting effects in the background. *Cottonwood Rhapsody #1* (page 27) used one version of this image. *Bird Thoughts II* (page 15) also used versions of this design. The top half of a very simplified version of this tree design was the basis for *Splendid Moment* (page 37).

> **TIP**
>
> Remember that the blending modes menu can be found under the *Normal* command in the upper left corner of the *Layers palette*, which is found on the right side of your screen. Alternatively, blending modes appear under *Layer>New Layer>Mode* in newer versions of Photoshop Elements.

Original photo shot, Deidre's cottonwood tree, through screen and window

Version 1: *Cutout filter* applied, colors exaggerated by successive applications of *Cutout filter* and *Auto Smart Fix (Enhance>Auto Smart Fix)*

Version 3: *Cutout* version stacked on top of orange-purple gradient with *Difference blend*

Version 2: *Cutout* version stacked on top of original with *Exclusion blend*

Version 4: Version 3 with a second layer of the original photo on top with *Exclusion blend*

Sunset sky, unaltered photo

Version 5: Original tree and sunset sky stacked with *Difference blend*—similar to one used in *Cottonwood Rhapsody #1* (page 27)

Version 6: Tree and sunset sky stacked with *Exclusion blend*

Version 7: Top half of *Cutout* version layered with a *Gradient* and a black-and-white *Invert* of the same image used in *Splendid Moments* (page 37)

robins

The various robin images used in the quilts *Return of the Robins* (page 49) and *Birds in the Bush* (page 76) look complex after color changes, resulting in very different images from the original and producing a painted quality in the images. Although complex to describe, most of these variations were arrived at by playing around and then saving the images that I liked.

The order of the five layers creating Version 1 is summarized here. Similar layers were created and are shown in the accompanying photos.

Fourth layer: Turquoise sky with exaggerated color, *Saturation, Darken blend*

Third layer: Light lavender, *Gradient fill, Difference blend*

Second layer: Robin 1, with *Difference blend*

First layer: Robin 2, with *Difference blend*

Background layer: Robin 3

Robin image 1

Robin image 2, cropped and enlarged

Robin image 3, cropped and enlarged again

Three robin images, stacked, with *Overlay blend* shown for illustration purposes

Turquoise cloudy sky image, top layer in stack, with *Darken blend*

Version 1: Blue stacked robin image

The blue stacked robin image in Version 1 served as the basis for several color change variations in *Return of the Robins* (page 49). By adding a different layer of sky photograph in each case and blending with the *Difference blend* mode, an unexpected bright image resulted.

Version 1: Blue stacked robin image

Pink and blue sky added on top of stack

Resulting Version 2: Final green and pink robins against sunset sky achieved with *Difference blend*

Cropped section of blue stacked robins

Cropped section of background skyline

Version 3: Resulting pale close-up robin with mountain skyline, achieved with *Difference blend*

Cropped single robin

Pink gradation part of sky

Version 4: Resulting red and green robin with *Difference blend*

Use More Complex Techniques

Now you can try your hand at creating more complicated images. Use four or more layers, each with a different blending mode, and perhaps a different filter. In addition to the ideas below, look at the quilts in the Gallery (pages 72–87) for more ideas and examples.

SOME THINGS TO TRY

The basic principles of photo editing were covered in Chapters 5, 6, and 7. Apply them here. Additionally, topics are indexed at the end of the book (see page 95 for further information). Remember there are no wrong choices, just endless design possibilities!

■ Duplicate images into several layers with different transformations on each layer and different blending modes.

■ Combine one background photograph with several different photos, or select one top photo and use several different backgrounds.

■ Repeat an image by selecting it, enlarging it, and moving a copy to a different location in your design frame. Do this more than once and in different sizes.

■ Invert an image, and combine it with itself or others.

■ Enlarge and crop portions of your design, and layer these with others.

■ Add layers that were created by sketch filters or exaggerated edge filters.

■ Flip part of the image to create a mirror image, and paste it into your design. (*Image>Rotate>Flip Horizontal* or *Vertical*).

■ Scan some of your own drawings, dyed fabrics, or painting experiments, and use them as layers in your digital constructions.

■ Use more than one filter on a photo.

■ Try sharpening your photos excessively before applying other filters.

Organize Your Design Work

Decide how you would like to keep track of your digital experiments at the computer. Store them in folders on the computer with names that allow you to find them again. Once they have been used in a quilt, store copies in a folder with the quilt's name and date. Also keep copies of the original photos in these folders.

You may also find it helpful to keep a notebook of design ideas printed out with notes, comments, or other sketches. And you may want to do actual cut-and-paste paper collages with some of the digital designs, just as you did with the photo collage journal.

As you gain experience with the simple changes, you will find many more interesting effects can be produced by combining techniques. You will start to think of your computer as a canvas with which you can construct your own paintings to go into your quilt designs. Combining many photographs or portions of photographs, changing colors, changing values, inverting, reflecting, repeating images, and changing the way the layers interact will all result in unique expressions for your artwork. What follows is a gallery of quilts with examples of some of the imagery that was used in each quilt and notes on how the digital transformations were achieved. Try these with your own photographs.

gallery

The Gallery Quilts demonstrate the techniques introduced in Chapters 5, 6, and 7. Photo-editing topics are indexed (see page 95) for further reference.

BLUE HILLS

Blue Hills celebrates one of my favorite walks along an Open Space trail. There is a lovely little old barn, long empty and very charming. There are lots of grasses (and cows). And there are many old cottonwood trees. Several of the images used in this quilt include photos layered with a scanned watercolor that I did. The watercolor layer not only gives a color change but adds a nice painting texture to the prints. The *Cutout filter,* heavily applied to a photo of a grove of trees and blended with *Difference blend*, transformed this rather dull original photo into something much more interesting.

Blue Hills, 53″ × 34″, 2005

Painted cheesecloth addition

Cow and tree color changes (described on pages 60–61)

Blue watercolor layered over *Cutout* tree with *Difference blend* and a *Gradient layer*

Stretched tree and barn print

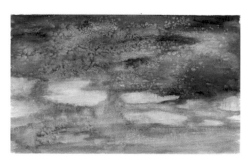

Original tree and barn image with *Cutout filter* applied

Original grove of trees photo

Scanned watercolor used as layer with *Cutout* tree image and *Cutout* grove of trees

Blue watercolor layered over repeated *Cutout filter* applied to image of grove of trees with *Overlay blend*

WEST ARAPAHOES AT SUNSET

I take many pictures of our mountains to the west. Several panoramas of sky views with exaggerated color were used as the backgrounds. Tree silhouettes, elk, and a landscape with the *Embossed filter* were added with varying *Opacity* settings. Some of the sky imagery is dye-painted fabric; one image has tree branches printed over it to repeat the image used in one of the photo prints.

Blue and green trees appliquéd onto print

West Arapahoes at Sunset, 58″ × 40″, 2005

Image with pale trees, dark elk, and *Emboss filter* used on layers containing mountains and one tree

Aspen photo layered with part of mountain background with color change

Another sky view with *Emboss filter* used on tree and mountains

Original photo of aspen tree in winter

Aspen tree branches after sketchily erasing the background, leaving pixels behind for an imperfect look. I used the *Magic Wand* selection tool with a small tolerance level to imperfectly select the branches and leaves.

BIRDS IN THE BUSH

Starting with three photos (a tree silhouette with a vague mountain background, an image of peeling paint, and a stormy sky photo, used with a copy of itself) plus the robin image discussed on page 69, I developed the imagery in *Birds in the Bush*. Four strips of varying widths made up the background. The top strip was an image of peeling paint combined with the stormy sky image. The middle strip had one small tree, the peeling paint, and the two stormy skies. The bottom strip had four layers:

Third layer: The trees with *Darken blend*

Second layer: Stormy sky repeat with *Difference blend*

First layer: Peeling paint photo with *Difference blend*

Background layer: Stormy sky

I greatly enlarged a copy of the tree, stretched it vertically, and combined it with the backgrounds (in the computer design). Then I divided the whole design into four strips for printing. I added the dark blue dyed strips and applied the robin rectangles.

Birds in the Bush, 30˝ × 46˝, 2006

Original photo of tree and mountains

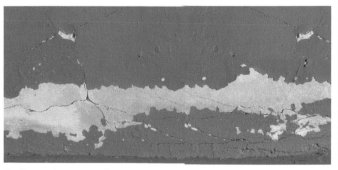

Peeling paint on a wall

Stormy sky photo

Trees photo layered with peeling paint using *Darken blend*

Trees, peeling paint, and two copies of stormy sky, combined as described on the previous page

CRANES AND CLOUDS

I made a series of quilts on the theme of sandhill cranes flying through an exotic sky. With digital techniques you can create your own exotic sky without having actually photographed one. The background layer of charmeuse silk was printed with billowing golden-reddish clouds and sky. This sky was created by layering a portion of diffuse blue sky over a repeated image of billowing clouds from another photo. (The repeated cloud image was created by pasting two copies of the billowing clouds side by side.) The trees in the rectangles were created using the inverted tree silhouettes derived from the one lone tree shown on page 51.

The order of the layers for the tree and cloud print is as follows:

Third layer: Diffuse blue sky with *Difference blend*

Second layer: Inverted trees outlines with *Normal blend*

First layer: Blue color fill with *Lighten blend*

Background layer: Repeated billowing cloud layer

I applied the rectangles with free-motion zigzag. The cranes were printed separately, appliquéd, and quilted.

Cranes and Clouds #3, 41″ × 12″, 2007

Repeated billowing clouds

Background sky print

Printed fabric for cut rectangles

Inverted tree silhouette layer

Top two layers: Diffuse sky with *Difference blend* with trees layer underneath

HARMONY

This quilt was constructed from one large digital design, which was divided into three pieces and printed on silk before being quilted and stitched together slightly offset. The top layer is the rock face, which adds a grainy look, and the crack, which resembles a mountain outline. This layer changes the color of the under layers.

The fourth layer is similar to the tree silhouettes used in the *Cranes and Cloud* series (pages 78–79). The third and second layers use the same photo of a bird at the bird feeder, caught fanning its wings. The bird photo was copied and rotated in the third layer. Each copy was treated differently in the blending modes to give a slightly different look. The mountain skyline and the *Gradient fill* compose the first and background layers.

Harmony, 50″ × 13″, 2007

Fifth layer: Top layer, rock face, *Pin Light blend*

All layers combined

Fourth layer: Tree silhouettes, *Exclusion blend*

Second and third layers: Left bird, *Hard Light blend;* right bird *Darken blend*

First layer: Mountain skyline, *Difference blend*

Background layer: Blue *Gradient fill,* reflected from center

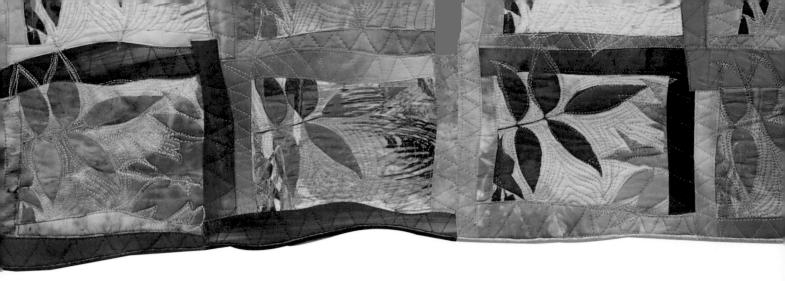

Ash Splash

Thirty-nine rectangles became *Ash Splash*. Each rectangle is composed of the same photo of ash leaves combined with various background layers and *Color fill* layers to achieve many, many color variations of the same image. It is a good example of using a simple, not very interesting photo to achieve wonderful digital images. Looking at the captions, you can see that the two leaf images, their backgrounds, and a *Color fill* were used in different orders and with different *Blending modes* to produce all the elements. Some leaves were cut from painted fabric and appliquéd for larger and more dramatic effect and to reach over the borders.

Ash Splash, 56˝ × 38˝, 2005

Original multiple leaf photo

Water ripples photo with *Cutout filter*

Resulting image: Third layer, selected leaves, *Normal blend;* second layer, pink *Color fill, Difference blend;* first layer, water ripples *Normal blend;* background layer, original leaves photo

Leaves selected with background erased

Original cloud photo

Resulting image: Third layer, selected leaves, *Difference blend;* second layer, clouds, *Difference blend;* first layer, yellow-orange *Color fill, Exclusion blend;* background layer, original leaves photo

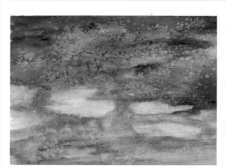

Original scan of watercolor painting

Third layer: Selected leaves with *Overlay blend;* second layer, original leaves photo, *Difference blend;* first layer, watercolor with *Difference blend;* background layer, red color fill

MIGRATION DREAM #1

This quilt demonstrates the result of lots of computer play and printing experimentation. I used a simple original photograph (taken from the car early one January morning on my way to a workshop) and cropped, stretched, and applied the *Cutout filter*. Then I flipped a duplicate of that result, both vertically and horizontally, and used it as the second layer. With a watercolor experiment added in, a photo of an ancient ruin as a supplemental print, and a color *Gradient fill*, I produced many colorways.

I composed the entire design on the computer at a size of 15 × 20 inches and a resolution of 180 ppi. I printed portions of the original digital design (with layers flattened) on different fabrics: silk charmeuse, silk noil, and pima cotton, and then patched them together. The different layers for the overall print design are as follows:

Fourth layer: Frosty morning photo with tree in left lower corner with *Darken blend*

Third layer: Frosty morning photo flipped horizontally and vertically with tree upside down in upper right, *Cutout filter*, *Difference blend*

Second layer: Black and white *Gradient fill*, *Difference blend*

First layer: Copy of the background layer, the watercolor scan, *Overlay blend*

Background layer: Original watercolor scan

Migration Dream #1, 36˝ × 28˝, 2007

Original photograph

Watercolor layer

Cropped, stretched, *Cutout filter* applied; layered with flipped version of itself

Overall print design

Supplemental photo lightly layered (40% opacity) and positioned over castle-like image in center resulting from watercolor

One printed panel

MIGRATION DREAM #2

This quilt uses some of the same prints on silks and cottons as in *Migration Dream #1* (pages 84–85), but it also features experimental images printed over metallic washes of textile acrylics, which resisted the inks slightly in some places and allowed the brush strokes to show through in other places. Images were also printed on silk organza of several densities and layered on top in some areas. The result is a mix of textural and reflective contrasts. Some cranes were printed, and some were appliquéd.

Migration Dream #2, 32" × 20", 2007

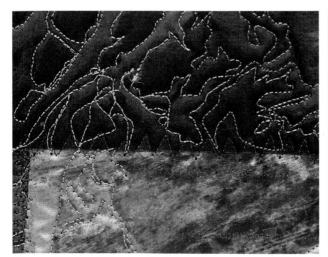

Note silver metallic paint undercoat.

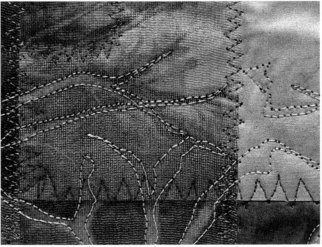

Note use of organza overlays.

constructing
the artwork

Most of the artworks presented in this book are art quilts. Obviously, much of what has been discussed would apply to many mixed media and collage artworks, although different considerations for construction would be needed. All of the previous layers of design decisions (photographic images, types of digital alteration, choice of fabric on which to print) are part of making the art, but you still have many additional design decisions to make if you want to create quilts. Although you can make quilts using traditional quilting techniques, you are not limited to those construction methods. What follows are some alternative construction techniques that I have used.

using the
design wall

You may decide to do your design work on the computer and determine exactly where each piece you have printed will be positioned. Or you may prefer a more improvisational approach, making decisions and changes as you design your piece.

Summer Heat computer design arrangement

Printed panel for *Summer Heat*

Printed panel for *Summer Heat*

Summer Heat #1, 44˝ × 28˝, 2003

When you use a design wall, start to arrange your printed fabric so that you see the developing artwork as it will be hung. Visualize the process as a collage: layer your printed images and other fabrics. Subtract and add fabrics and images. Layer cut-outs from the prints. Use transparent fabrics over background prints. It is tempting to consider all your prints as precious, not wanting to cut into them and wanting to use each and every one of them. You will have more freedom if you consider them part of your stash of fabrics, to be used only as needed. Make several different arrangements of your chosen elements, and photograph these different versions to decide which is most effective.

As you arrange your composition, make other design decisions, such as whether you want to enhance your work with painting, stamping, colored pencils, iron-on foiling, and so on. Many of these enhancements need to be done before the quilt is assembled and quilted.

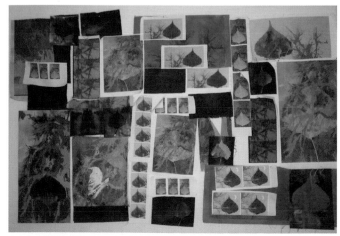

Design wall composition for *Cottonwood Rhapsody IV*

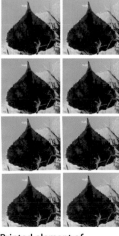

Printed element of *Cottonwood Rhapsody IV*

Printed element of *Cottonwood Rhapsody IV*

Cottonwood Rhapsody IV, 52″ × 38″, 2004

making the quilt

When you are satisfied with the composition, start to assemble it. Using fusible web, such as WonderUnder or Misty Fuse, or fusible batting makes this an easy process. Fusing, rather than piecing, allows more freedom in the arrangements and in the edges. You can cut a jagged outline or an erratically curved edge more easily when the fabric is backed with fusing and you don't have to worry about sewing together irregular pieces. Silks are much easier to handle when using some kind of fusing technique because fusible webs add firmness to the hand of the fabric.

Having taken a digital photograph of the composition, you can carefully disassemble it and take it to the ironing board or fusing table. (I have a large padded surface for fusing and pressing on one of my work tables.) If you want an especially puffy look after quilting, sew a print directly (without any fusing) to a non-fusible batting or a background fabric. The quilt stitching will give you a puffier effect than the quilt stitching on fused layers gives you.

You can assemble your quilt in the traditional way, laying the assembled top onto batting and backing fabric, then quilting it. Alternatively, you can do the quilt in sections, as described on the following page.

butting together mini-quilts

To build up a large quilt, you can create mini-quilts and attach them together after they are quilted. The stitching that holds them together can be quite visible and thus becomes a design element. Do this stitching with an extra fused strip on the back side of the seam for added stability. A fused strip on the front can serve as a sashing or lattice between two prints, as in *Virginia Creeper Vines* (shown on this page). Attach one quilted section to the next in a row, and then attach the entire row to the previous row, each time fusing a strip that is about ¾″ wide behind the attaching stitching, and/or adding a fused lattice strip on top as well.

Attaching mini-quilts together

Partially completed quilt

On these small mini-quilts, I do all or most of the quilting and decorative stitching while they are still small and easy to handle. Very little quilting or embellishment stitching is done once the entire quilt is constructed.

Quilting *Virginia Creeper Vines* mini-quilt section

adding quilted layers

For even more depth, you can add layers of quilted images. On the *Virginia Creeper Vines* quilt, an added layer is composed of the vines that are printed, fused to black wool felt on top of fusible black cotton interfacing, and quilted with black free-motion machine embroidery before being sewn down to the main quilt.

Virginia Creeper Vines, 39″ × 48″, 2008

stitching tells a story

In most of my quilts I use free-motion quilting as a layer of drawn lines on top of the images. My trusty Bernina helps me outline and echo the lines and shapes in the images. Sometimes the stitching is a layer of alternate line imagery and adds another element to the story. In *Rusted and Abandoned* the cross-stitches, done by hand, were added for a touch of hominess, perhaps part of what was abandoned.

Hand stitching on *Rusted and Abandoned*

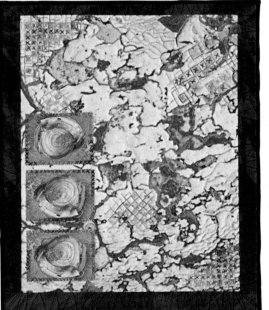

Rusted and Abandoned, 37˝ × 16˝, 2002

embellishing

When considering embellishments, you need to think about how easy it will be to sew on them or around them. Beads, heavy-thread hand stitching, or found objects usually need to be added after the quilting is done. In particular, beads are hard to sew around, so they generally come last. Paints and iron-on foils are usually added before the machine stitching/quilting so that you can stitch close to them or on them. Paints can also be added after all the stitching is done if you want to cover up the stitches under the paint. In the beaded quilt, *Red Admiral Wings,* the original photo used for the beading surface was a cropped and then posterized (page 55) image. The *Posterize filter* created more definite lines, shapes, and a reduced number of colors, which corresponded to the beading design decisions.

Original cropped butterfly photo

Posterized image as base for beading

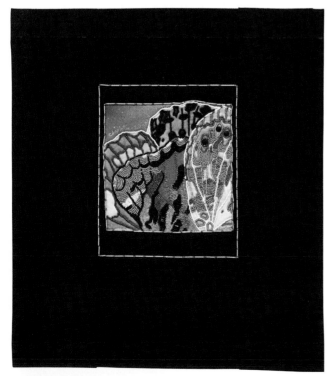

Red Admiral Wings, 17″ × 19″, 2004

the final layer —lightfast considerations

The very last layer of your quilt is the acrylic UV resistant spray or the UV protection acrylic varnish. Although the pigment inks that I use are more lightfast than the dye-based inks of most desktop printers, I like to add as much protection as possible. More information on the testing of these types of protection for inkjet prints can be found on the Golden paints website (see Resources, page 94). See also page 41 in the Chapter 4 discussion of post-treatments.

I hope this book has inspired you to play with your photographs using Photoshop Elements. May you persist even when the computer gremlins attack, and may you find this artistic tool as much fun as I do.

"We do not stop playing because we grow old; we grow old because we stop playing." —George Bernard Shaw

recommended resources

Books about Photography and Mixed Media Uses of Photography

Airey, Theresa. *Digital Photo Art: Transform Your Images with Traditional & Contemporary Art Techniques*. New York: Lark Books, 2005.

Cartwright, Angela. *Mixed Emulsions.* Beverly: Quarry Books, 2007.

Finn, David. *How to Look at Everything.* New York: Harry N. Abrams, 2000.

Patterson, Freeman. *Photography and the Art of Seeing.* Toronto: Key Porter Books, 2004.

Schminke, Karin, Dorothy Simpson Krause, and Bonny Pierce Lhotka. *Digital Art Studio: Techniques for Combining Inkjet Printing with Traditional Art Materials.* New York: Watson-Guptil, 2004.

Books about Quilts Using Photographic Imagery

Fallert, Caryl Bryer. *Quilt Savvy: Fallert's Guide to Images on Fabric.* Paducah: American Quilter's Society, 2004.

Hansen, Gloria. *Digital Essentials: The Quilt Makers Must-Have Guide to Images, Files, and More.* Bowling Green: Electric Quilt Company, 2008.

Hewlett-Packard Company with Cyndy Lyle Rymer and Lynn Koolish. *More Photo Fun: Exciting New Ideas for Printing on Fabric for Quilts & Crafts.* Lafayette: C&T Publishing, 2005.

Meech, Sandra. *Contemporary Quilts: Design, Surface and Stitch.* London: B. T. Batsford, 2003.

Rymer, Cyndy Lyle, with Lynn Koolish. *Innovative Fabric Imagery for Quilts.* Lafayette: C&T Publishing, 2007.

Wheeler, Beth, with Lori Marquette. *Altered Photo Artistry.* Lafayette: C&T Publishing, 2007.

Books and DVDs about Using Photoshop Elements

Ashford, Janet, and John Odam. *Start with a Scan: A Guide to Transforming Scanned Photos and Objects into High Quality Art.* Berkeley: Peachpit Press, 1996.

Beardsworth, John. *Blending Modes Cookbook for Digital Photographers.* Sebastopol: O'Reilly Media , 2005.

Collandre, Patrick et al. *Creating Photomontages with Photoshop: A Designer's Notebook.* Sebastopol: O'Reilly Media, 2005.

Georges, Gregory. *50 Fast Digital Photo Techniques*. Hoboken: Wiley Publishing, 2005.

Koolish, Lynn. *Lynn Koolish Teaches You Printing on Fabric,* DVD. Lafayette: C&T Publishing, 2008.

Odam, John. *Start with a Digital Camera.* Berkeley: Peachpit Press, 2003.

Pring, Roger. *Filter Effects Encyclopedia.* Sebastopol: O'Reilly Media, 2005.

Shelbourne, Tim. *Photo Effects Cookbook.* Sebastopol: O'Reilly Media, 2005.

Sullivan, Michael J. *Make Your Scanner a Great Design and Production Tool.* Cincinnati: North Light Books, 1998.

Books about Creativity

Cameron, Julia. *The Artist's Way.* New York: Tarcher/Perigee Books, 1992.

Leland, Nita. *The Creative Artist.* Cincinnati: North Light Books, 2006.

Maisel, Eric. *Fearless Creating.* New York: Tarcher/Putnam, 1995.

Websites

www.ctpub.com

Photoshop Elements Basics (look for *Tips & Techniques for Quiltmaking & More* under *Consumer Resources*). Also find other C&T books about digital photos and quilts.

www.adobe.com/downloads

Thirty-day trial version of Photoshop Elements 6. Check availability pending launch of Photoshop Elements 7.

www.inkAID.com

Source for inkAID precoatings

www.cjenkinscompany.com

Source of Bubble Jet 2000 and information on the two types of printer inks (also check out Jerome's column)

www.bryerpatch.com

Good information about printing on fabric

www.peachpit.com

Articles from its authors and how-tos

www.goldenpaints.com

Source of Golden Digital Grounds and Archival Aerosol MSA Varnish with UVLS

www.krylon.com

UV–Resistant Clear Acrylic Coating and Preserve It! (under Paper Finishes)

www.broderbund.com

Source of The Print Shop software

Pretreated Fabric Sheets

ColorPlus Inkjet Fabrics by Color Textiles

Many different fabrics, including poplin, broadcloth, denim, and silks in various size sheets and rolls

Check the company's website to order online: www.colorplusfabrics.com.

EQ Printables by Electric Quilt

A variety of cotton sheets in 8½″ × 11″, 11″ × 17″, and 13″ × 19″ sizes

Check the company's website for retailers, or order online: www.electricquilt.com.

Print N' Create by Pellon

Cotton sheets in sew-on, iron-on, and peel-and-stick versions. Available at many quilt and fabric stores or online: www.shoppellon.com

Printed Treasures by Milliken

Cotton sheets in sew-on, iron-on, and peel-and-stick versions. Available at many quilt and fabric stores or online: www.printedtreasures.com

Inkjet Printing Sheets by Jacquard

Cotton, silk, and ExtravOrganza sheets. Check the company's website for retail locations: www.jacquardproducts.com.

Dharma Trading Co.

Pretreated fabric sheets in silk and cotton. Dharma also offers Jacquard Inkjet Fabric Systems complete selection of 90 inkjet-ready fabrics, in widths from 17″ to 58″ wide.

Order online from their website: www.dharmatrading.com.

Natural Miracle Fabric Sheets by C. Jenkins Necktie & Chemical Co.

Cotton in sheets and by the yard, freezer paper carrier sheets, and Bubble Jet Set and Rinse. Order online from the company's website: www.cjenkinscompany.com.

about the author

work has appeared in many books and magazines. After many years working principally as a weaver of tapestries, she began to make quilts and currently concentrates on creating digital imagery printed on fabric and assembled into quilt art.

When not working in the digital darkroom in her sunny quilting studio, she can be found knitting and listening to classical music, hiking in the mountains with her camera, sitting in the audience at an opera performance, or trying to tame her messy, leafy garden. Her experience as an artist-in-residence in Rocky Mountain National Park remains a strong influence. More of her work can be seen on her website at www.charlotteziebarth.com.

Charlotte was born in Chicago and raised in the Midwest, went to school at Montana State University in Bozeman and the University of Colorado in Boulder, and now considers herself a westerner. She has lived with her husband, Ken, in Boulder, Colorado, for more than thirty-five years. They have a daughter, Jennifer, and a new granddaughter, Laurel.

Although Charlotte has a background in academic psychology, she has worked with art and cloth most of her life as a dyer, weaver, clothing designer, knitter, and quilter. Passion for the fiber arts steered her toward working full time in art, setting aside her academic career. Widely exhibited and collected, her

index

For a list of other fine books from C&T Publishing, ask for a free catalog:

C&T Publishing, Inc.

P.O. Box 1456

Lafayette, CA 94549

(800) 284-1114

Email: ctinfo@ctpub.com

Website: www.ctpub.com

C&T Publishing's professional photography services are now available to the public. Visit us at www.ctmediaservices.com.

For quilting supplies:

Cotton Patch

1025 Brown Ave.

Lafayette, CA 94549

Store: (925) 284-1177

Mail order: (925) 283-7883

Email: CottonPa@aol.com

Website: www.quiltusa.com

Great Titles *from* C&T PUBLISHING

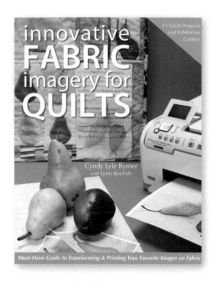
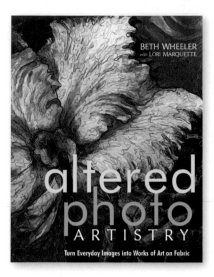
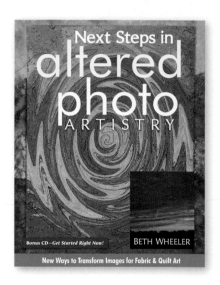
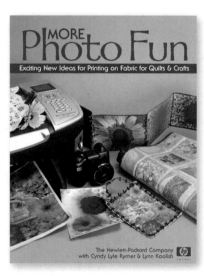
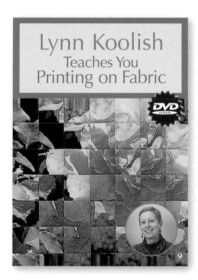